RUNNING WITH ROBOTS

REASONING WITH ROBOTS

RUNNING WITH ROBOTS

The American High School's
Third Century

Greg Toppo and Jim Tracy

The MIT Press
Cambridge, Massachusetts
London, England

The MIT Press would like to thank the anonymous peer reviewers who provided comments on drafts of this book. The generous work of academic experts is essential for establishing the authority and quality of our publications. We acknowledge with gratitude the contributions of these otherwise uncredited readers.

The authors would like to acknowledge that the title of this book was inspired by *The Second Machine Age: Work, Progress, and Prosperity in a Time of Brilliant Technologies* by Erik Brynjolfsson and Andrew McAfee.

This book was set in Stone Serif and Pangram by Jen Jackowitz. Printed and bound in the United States of America.

Library of Congress Cataloging-in-Publication Data

Names: Toppo, Greg, author. | Tracy, Jim, 1961- author.
Title: Running with robots : the American high school's third century / Greg Toppo and Jim Tracy.
Description: Cambridge, Massachusetts : The MIT Press, 2021. | Includes bibliographical references and index.
Identifiers: LCCN 2020040685 | ISBN 9780262045896 (hardcover)
Subjects: LCSH: Artificial intelligence—Educational applications—United States. | Education, Secondary—United States. | Education—Effect of technological innovations on—United States.
Classification: LCC LB1028.3 .T67 2021 | DDC 373.73—dc23
LC record available at https://lccn.loc.gov/2020040685

10 9 8 7 6 5 4 3 2 1

To Julie
To Jan

CONTENTS

PROLOGUE: WELCOME TO THAMES ACADEMY

In this book, we argue that the revolution being wrought by accelerating advances in artificial intelligence, machine learning, and robotics necessitates equally dramatic new pedagogies, some of which our teachers have yet to invent.

In succeeding chapters, we'll visit schools where these changes are already beginning to take root. But to better illustrate the full scope of what's possible, and what must take place, let's engage in a time-honored thought experiment of "looking backward" to imagine what could be in the near future.[1] In our case, a somnolent Massachusetts high school principal—let's call him Rumple—falls asleep late one afternoon in January 2020. He awakes to find that he has, astonishingly, slept straight though the intervening twenty years. It is the year 2040.

He emerges from his secluded home one spring morning to find that the neighborhood hasn't changed much, aside from the strange little cars in everyone's driveways. In his own driveway, the faded blue Honda Accord that's forever burning oil is gone, replaced by (and he's not really sure how it got there) a vehicle the size and approximate shape of a double-wide lounge chair with a gently curving roof.

Not exactly sure how long he has been asleep, Rumple does the first thing that comes to mind: he skips the strange car and walks to his old familiar school, just a few blocks away.

Like the neighborhood, the high school seems to have changed little. It's still a solid, three-story, red brick edifice at the heart of a residential area, though a sign on the front door now reads "Winterville THAMES Academy." Not quite sure what to make of this—the Thames River is in England, thousands of miles away—he pulls on the massive door, anticipating that, as always, it'll be locked. To his surprise, it opens easily. "Hmm, they've really let security lapse," he says to himself.

What he doesn't know is that he has just activated an automated infrared/X-ray/iris scanner. By the time Rumple walks the several steps to the spot where his old office used to be, the system has silently identified him as an unarmed, middle-aged male, previously unregistered, no prior school contact—he's rated "harmless," with a 72 percent probability he's a visiting grandparent. The system returns a 24 percent probability he's there to complain about kids on his property, a 4 percent probability he's lost.

He stands at the front office, but no one is there to greet him. As he looks around for the receptionist, a pleasant but disembodied female voice says, "Welcome," while a device resembling an ATM issues a thin plastic sticker that reads, "Two-Hour Pass—Restricted." He pulls the sticker from the machine and pats it onto his chest. While he doesn't know it, the sticker will, if needed, limit which areas he can enter, triggering an alarm if he strays.

Moments later, he comes face-to-face with the principal—let's call her Bellamy—a woman in her late 30s with a ready smile and a firm handshake. She's standing there because her Oculus Everyday glasses alerted her to the unfamiliar old man in the vestibule and suggested she go meet him before he gets too far.

With the reader's permission, we'll skip over the moment of revelation, the scenes of amazement, of Rumple's dawning realization that it's 2040 and most of what he knew is gone or going fast. We'll only mention that Bellamy, the new principal, immediately recognized him and now, sitting across the couch from him in her office, informs him that she was, in fact, a former student of his, at this very high school, back when it was plain old Winterville High.

Over a bracing cup of coffee, he gets his bearings and soon realizes that he has stumbled upon something educators live their whole lives dreaming about: the ability to see not only how their own work has turned out but how schools, students, and teachers have changed over a generation—for better or worse.

Bellamy, sensing that he's lost in thought, tries to bring him back to the "present."

"I graduated in the spring of 2020—just a few months after you . . . fell asleep."

"You did?"

"Indeed," she says.

Rumple snaps out of his reverie—like most good teachers, he has a kind of deep, if imperfect, memory for his former students. And, of course, hers was the last class he remembers. Once he realizes who Bellamy is, he recalls that she had aspirations to major in computer science.

"You were going to work in tech—I remember you were smitten with Silicon Valley," he says.

"Yes, exactly!" she answers, pleased that he remembered.

"So . . . how did you end up here, back in your hometown—as a high school principal?"

"Well, some things don't work out as planned, which sometimes is a very good thing. It's a long story."

Just then, Bellamy's glasses remind her that it is almost lunchtime, and she offers to take Rumple out for a hot meal.

"I'll let my assistant know I'm taking a long lunch," she says as they rise. They walk through the unoccupied outer office and Bellamy says in a loud, clear voice, "I won't be back for a while, Annie. Could you please call for my car? Also, can you reschedule my afternoon appointments?" A green light above the door blinks and that familiar, disembodied female voice says, "Your car is on the way. Your appointments have been rescheduled. Have a good afternoon, Dr. Bellamy."

"*Doctor* Bellamy, eh?" Rumple queries approvingly, impressed. Bellamy smiles with a mixture of pride and humility.

"Yes, well . . ."

"Don't forget," the disembodied voice interrupts, "you also have a series of parent meetings beginning at 9 a.m. tomorrow and a Friday deadline for a grant proposal that is 62 percent complete. Based on past successful applications, your proposal currently has a 23 percent probability of being funded. Would you like to hear a few ways to improve it now?"

"No, thank you, Annie," she says, taking Rumple by the arm and leading him through the door. "Have a nice afternoon."

"Thank you. I'll send those suggestions as an addendum to my previous memo. Have a nice afternoon."

Rumple looks behind them to see the office lights dim.

"Your assistant?"

"She keeps me on track, but she can be a bit . . . solicitous," Bellamy says. "I need to tweak her helpfulness settings. She's killing my long-term memory."

At the curb, almost as soon as they approach, a tiny self-driving car appears, much like the ones Rumple saw when he first ventured forth from his home. They climb in, travel several blocks, and soon arrive at a brightly lit neighborhood restaurant with inviting outdoor seating. Once they emerge from the car, it beeps once and drives off.

"Self-parking," Bellamy says.

"Amazing," Rumple says as he watches the car roll down the block and disappear around a corner.

A greeter welcomes them warmly and asks Bellamy how her family is, then guides them to an outdoor table and disappears. They take a seat and, though it's only just noon, Bellamy surmises that Rumple's morning might call for a drink or two. She clears her throat and says, "Could we have a lime seltzer and . . . ?" she looks at Rumple. "What are you drinking?"

"Um, scotch," he says. "On the rocks."

"Scotch on the rocks—make it a Macallan Twelve-Year. Oh, and an order of your antipasto," Bellamy says.

Rumple blinks. "Who are you talking to?"

"The kitchen," she says, pointing to a pulsing, green-lit button situated next to a microphone embedded in the table. She pushes the button and it turns red. Seconds later, a tiny automated cart sidles up to the table. She removes the glass, hands it to Rumple, then lifts out a glass bottle of seltzer for herself and toasts their health. Rumple takes a substantial swallow of scotch and places the glass on the table.

"Amazing," he says. Just then another cart arrives, carrying a large plate of Italian meats, cheeses, olives, pickled vegetables, and a small loaf of bread.

"The bread here is addictive," Bellamy says. "They make it in house." She lifts the plate and the robot cart speeds off. As he watches it round a corner, Rumple recalls that Bellamy had said she'd worked in tech after graduation.

"Oh yes," she says. "I studied computer engineering. I spent four years after college at Apple, teaching Siri—remember her?—how to more accurately suggest to users where to buy an upright piano or a ripe dragon fruit. The problems were delightful—try teaching a bot the difference between Elvis and Elvish—but the work, to be blunt, got dull. I left and went to grad school to study history."

"History? Good god, I studied history!" Rumple says, the scotch taking the chill off his singular morning.

"I loved it, but my parents were not amused," Bellamy says. "They thought tech was the living end. They'd spent years reading about how we'd soon need fewer teachers, how online learning would make us all obsolete. But I saw that a shift was happening. As much as all of us in tech believed that we could solve every problem with the brute force of data and computing, I knew we'd always need teachers—maybe just not the same kinds of teachers."

Rumple fears what's coming next and takes a large slug of his drink, but Bellamy changes the subject: "In grad school, I studied nineteenth- and early twentieth-century industrialization," she says. "It changed how we worked and where we lived. Even with all that time for workers to adjust—more than a century—the entire industrial era was fraught with conflict: the Populist revolt, union struggles, rapid urbanization, and massive immigration."

"Of course," Rumple says.

"And of course, in the late twentieth century, vast portions of the workforce shifted to service sector jobs."

"Yes," Rumple says. "I remember that. I *lived* through it. But please—I have to ask: What else happened after I dozed off?"

"Well, actually it happened before you dozed off," Bellamy says.

"Before? I remember the 2008 recession, but . . ."

"I hate to bring this up," Bellamy replies, biting her lip, "but do you remember 2016?"

"Yes, of course," Rumple says, then deflates slightly into his chair.

"I was just a high school first-year at the time," Bellamy says.

"'First-year'? You mean freshman?"

"We call them first-years now, sir," she says. "'Freshman' is considered insufficiently gender-inclusive. In any event, historians now agree that the rise of Donald Trump and his raw populist anger were largely a response to automation."

"Automation? You mean *immigration*."

"Oh no," she says, plucking an olive from the plate. "Automation."

"So, you're saying . . . *robots* brought us Trump?"

"You have to remember," Bellamy says, "American manufacturing jobs were disappearing, and millions of blue-collar workers were angry and bewildered. Even though unemployment was low at the time, those who were employed experienced decades of wage stagnation and insecurity."

"Yes, but . . ."

"Trump blamed immigrants and offshoring, of course, but these were responsible for just a fraction of all that. Here's the amazing thing: after the 2008 recession, manufacturing actually picked up. Demand for American-made goods rose in the decade before 2016. To meet the demand, manufacturers stepped up production."

"So why the anger?" Rumple asks.

"Well, manufacturing recovered, but the manufacturing job market didn't."

"I'm not sure I follow you."

"Companies increased production not by hiring more people, but by bringing in an ever-growing army of industrial robots. US companies were producing more goods than before, and they were doing it here—but with *fewer human workers*. I remember reading about a textile mill in North Carolina where fewer than 150 people did the work once done by 2,000. On the overnight shift, eleven people ran a facility as big as four soccer fields."[2]

"You mean football fields?" Rumple says.

"Oh no," Bellamy says. "American football was outlawed
years ago as inhumane—all those brain injuries to young
people. What a disaster! The United Nations eventually cat-
egorized the NFL as a human rights violator. It relocated to
Eastern Europe."

"Fascinating," he says.

"Indeed," she says. "But as many of us focused on industrial automation, a bigger crisis was taking hold, and it wasn't
on the factory floor. It was on the trading room floor, in the
pharmacy, the medical examination room, and the court-
room. It was in the newsroom, the psychiatrist's office, and
the attorney's conference room. While millions fretted about
robots replacing blue-collar workers, artificial intelligence and
machine learning began colonizing highly skilled, college-
educated, 'thinking' professions like ours. Digital technology began doing for brain work what the steam engine and
its descendants had done for muscle power. As technology
improved—and unlike human brain power, it has always
improved exponentially—its only limitation was the imagina-
tion of programmers, designers, and forward-thinking innovators within the professions themselves."

"I fear where this is going," Rumple says.

"Over the next few years—just the blink of an eye in historical terms—millions of college-educated white-collar workers saw their jobs transformed. Many workers reskilled, but
millions found themselves left behind, hustling to make ends
meet in jobs that had once been full-time but were suddenly
part-time, since many of the low-grade, routine, repetitive
tasks they'd always done were suddenly automated."

As he listens, Rumple can't help but look out the window.
He watches as dozens of those tiny, self-driving cars zoom by.
"You know," he says, "I just realized that in just the few hours
I've been, well, awake, I've seen four good middle-class service

jobs—receptionist, secretary, driver, and waiter—performed entirely by robots."

"Then you see my point," Bellamy replies. Sensing his despair, she adds, "Of course, technology almost always creates new kinds of jobs. It's true, robots brought our drinks and our appetizer, but they also freed up the restaurant owner to build and operate his own in-house bakery—mostly automated, of course—and spend more on high-quality ingredients."

"The bread *is* amazing," Rumple admits.

"All the same, the transition took years, with many false starts and stops."

"How bad was it?" Rumple asks.

"Well, imagine an economy in which the ranks of the blue-collar unemployed or underemployed swelled with the addition of white-collar workers—expensively educated millions who always assumed their 'knowledge economy' jobs would render them immune to technological obsolescence. The politics of anger took on a new scale altogether."

"Oh my," Rumple says. "Then what happened?"

"Do you really need to ask that?"

"Yes!" Rumple says, sitting forward in his chair. *"Please tell me: What happened?"*

Bellamy smiles. "Our education system came to the rescue—as it always does."

1   HISTORY COMES IN WAVES

In this book, we're going to look back almost exactly two centuries, to the very birth of the public high school in America in 1821, to try to understand what the next century may hold. For at least the past one hundred years, we have been educating students to prepare them for the knowledge economy. This was predicated upon one of the most basic assumptions of our civilization: information was scarce.

That assumption no longer holds.

Since the first humans stood upright, information has been difficult to acquire, even more difficult to aggregate, and exceedingly difficult to transfer intact intergenerationally. This made information precious and the archiving and preservation of it a fragile, almost sacred undertaking. It is no wonder that, architecturally, our libraries so often assume the vernacular of temples or cathedrals.

When a critical resource is scarce, vast cultural constructs tend to reflect the collective endeavor to optimize its use. In the case of material goods, for instance, humanity has inhabited a scarcity civilization for most of its time on earth. Until around 1900 in the more industrially advanced nations, humanity was unable to consistently produce more than marginally above sustenance levels. Only around 1900—and then only in the most economically advanced countries—was it possible to manufacture vast surpluses, bringing in the unprecedented economic challenge of overproduction.

Culture broadly reflected this shift. In the Victorian Era of the nineteenth century, for instance, high cultural premium was placed upon virtues such as self-control and delayed gratification, whether in the realm of finance, sexuality, or tippling. With the transition to a surplus productive capacity, a cultural shift took place along with the economic. In the 1890s, open discussion about fears of economic depressions due to over-production fed a new geopolitical expansionist rhetoric on the part of thinkers such as Alfred Thayer Mahan and leaders such as Teddy Roosevelt. Suddenly, the focus was on how to secure new markets for American products around the globe.

Out of this, an entire new industry, exemplified by Madison Avenue, emerged from the quaint foundations of what had constituted advertising, with a new, research-based approach to convince American domestic consumers to jettison Victorian-era consumption patterns in favor of the new mores of immediate gratification and conspicuous consumption. This became the dominant cultural and economic paradigm of twentieth-century America. (In some ways, the 1960s counterculture was not countercultural at all, but, rather, a consummate expression of consumption capitalism, with its emphasis upon fun, indulgence, and tuning in—but that is the subject for another book.)

Just as the twentieth century transformed humanity's relationship to material goods, so will the twenty-first century transform our relationship to—and cultural constructs around—information. In other words, we are in the very midst of coming to terms with a historically unprecedented era in which information is no longer a scarce and precious item but a ubiquitous commodity. Printed books are no longer the chief repositories of information; digital formats are. Humans are no longer the chief progenitors of data; today, the majority of information on the web is machine-generated, and that ratio is skewing steadily and ever more rapidly in favor of the machines.

This has meant a cultural and institutional revolution in content and knowledge curation that has scarcely begun to reach full impact. One example: until the end of the twentieth century, modern society had sufficiently limited data flows to allow for a well engineered regulation of how information was curated and given a cultural stamp of validation. Universities curated research-based information; newspapers and three major television networks controlled news, but also were held accountable by key public institutional stakeholders for the content they conveyed. All of that, of course, has been swept aside by the tsunami of information outlets today, some of the most spurious sort.

Our inherited cultural models for ensuring a modicum of validation and responsibility in news reporting have been, at least temporarily, overwhelmed by the tidal surge of new sources and delivery conduits. It will take some time for culture and responsible societal stakeholders to adjust and develop new delivery models appropriate to an era of information abundance.

Meanwhile, a small group of innovators in each information-heavy profession, largely unconstrained by habit or custom, has begun to rethink at an almost molecular level how work gets done.

The many ways in which this shift will affect our schools—and specifically our high schools—is the subject of this book.

The path we'll follow won't be unidirectional or even sequential—we'll start ("School Comes Through") as close as we can to the beginning, in the 1820s, just a few decades after the founding of the Republic. That's when early Americans—not just in New England but across the expanding nation—confronted a disruptive, high-tech revolution with an educational innovation of their own: the first free, taxpayer-supported public high school.

Next ("Illusion of Humanity"), we'll take a stab at understanding the new and quickly evolving world of artificial intelligence and how we as humans can begin processing the changes it is bringing.

Then ("The Trust Machine"), we'll look at how advances in technology are shaping our sense of connectedness, pushing us to rethink what students really want and need out of school—and what high school could look like if we simply shift our perspective and offer students what would seem like two contradictory things: more autonomy and more support.

We'll examine ("Robot Journalism, Robot Teaching") how machine learning and AI are already transforming our respective white-collar professions, and how practitioners in each must respond.

In between, we'll visit four schools that are confronting these challenges in different but equally enlightened ways:

- In Philadelphia ("What If School Were Real Life?"), an intensive, student-centered public magnet high school that draws students in every zip code in the city redefines what student agency can look like.

- In Iowa ("Don't Tell Me What You Want to Be When You Grow Up"), a small, experimental high school program is reinvigorating secondary education for students who had stopped seeing any usefulness or vitality in it.

- In New York City ("The Pyramids are Closed for Revolution"), a civics-focused high school hits upon a novel way to help its mostly low-income students focus on the future: world travel.

- Near Providence, Rhode Island, Jim's former employer ("*Festina Lente*, or Change Management at Rocky Hill School"), an independent day school steeped in tradition, undertakes a complete overhaul of its curriculum and its relationship to technology, pushing to make it more relevant and responsive to families.

Interestingly, not all of these schools are explicitly articulating their innovations as a direct response to AI and roboticization, but they are all emblematic of the imaginative reformulation of paideia in a milieu of transformation, at the root of which we can unerringly and consistently find the digital revolution, especially marked by AI going forward. None of these, of course, is a panacea with the full answer for educators, but they are all earnest and bold forays into the paradigmatic shifts we need for today's and tomorrow's schools.

We'll strike a note of caution ("Gimme Shelter") about the dark possibilities of AI while suggesting an antidote: a new humanities curriculum to prepare students to be wary of its dangers.

Finally ("A Post-Work World"), we look at the possibility that the near future could bring the end of work for most people. What might that look like? And what effect might it have on education?

In between each chapter, we'll briefly check in on our two educators, Rumple and Bellamy, as they tour classrooms in what's admittedly our rough-hewn vision of the high school of the future. They'll do their best to make sense of a world that is, by turns, both familiar and strange to early 2020s readers.

One easy-to-see result of the new information superabundance is the changed reality of a simple, nearly universal human act: reading. Twenty-five years ago, at the dawn of the World Wide Web, the critic Sven Birkerts posited that our changing information ecosystem had quietly brought us to the brink of "what may prove to be a kind of species mutation."[1] Reflecting on his own habits as well as those of his family, friends, and students, Birkerts observed what he termed "a deep transformation in the nature of reading, a shift from focused, sequential, text-centered engagement to a far more lateral kind of encounter." The web and its endlessly connected pages and media snacks had modified our reading habits seemingly overnight. In the place of "single-track concentration" arose "the restless, grazing behavior" of clicking and scrolling. "The electronic impulse," he wrote, "works against the durational reverie of reading."[2] We hope our readers will indulge us with the "durational reverie of reading" for what we consider to be the compelling and potentially decisive issues we address in this book. Education has historically been one of the institutional laggards in responding to broader societal change. Today's transition, however, warrants a sense of considerable urgency.

There have been two prior comparable technology-driven civilizational inflections in recorded human history: the Neolithic Revolution and the Industrial Revolution. The technological breakthrough on which the Neolithic rested was the domestication of grain. This revolutionary technology changed every dimension of human life and relations. Settled agriculture allowed for greater aggregations of people, giving rise to towns and cities, which gave rise to more complex social institutions—organized government, organized military systems, organized religious systems. The word "civilization" is related to *civitas*, the Latin word for city, and a customary convention is to date human civilization from the invention of the printed word, which emerged from the Egyptian state four millennia ago.

The Neolithic Revolution reached to the very core of human existential identity. Karl Jaspers once asked why Socrates, Buddha, Confucius, and Jesus happened to live within 500 years of one another. Perhaps the answer lies, in part, in the fact that, due to the agrarian Neolithic Revolution, population concentrations in various societies on the EuroAsian land mass during precisely this period were reaching critical mass. People were individuating from traditional cultural models that had previously subsumed the individual into earlier, smaller tribal identities. As people individuated, they sought new religious and ethical systems that could help mediate emergent ethical relationships between the individual and the collective.

The Neolithic Revolution transpired over the course of a millennium or more. The next great technology inflection, the Industrial Revolution, on the other hand, transpired on a more condensed timescale—over just one to two centuries. Predicated on the technological innovation of harnessing steam power, the Industrial Revolution was at least as thoroughgoing as the Neolithic, its effects rippling through the entire fabric of human experience and society just as the earlier transformation had. It is unmistakably clear that the implications of the Industrial Revolution included (but were far from limited to) rapid urbanization and population growth; global imperialism (followed by postcolonial revolutions); the upheavals exemplified by the revolutions of 1848, the American Civil War, the First World War, the Second World War; and Marxist Communism, to name but a few. These could not possibly have transpired as they did except under the press of forces unleashed globally by industrialization.

Industrialized nations have seen similar shifts in relatively recent history. The United States workforce, for instance, shifted from a preponderantly agrarian to a largely manufacturing base from the eighteenth to the nineteenth century, and then, again, to a predominantly service economy in the late twentieth century.

To use a phrase born near the beginning of the current revolution, let's fast-forward to today. One of the most pressing problems associated with our relationship to the changes that the information revolution poses, both for education and for jobs, is our temptation to downplay just how significant it is. Pundits argue that today's technology revolution (including its impact on jobs) is nothing we haven't seen before. They're right—we have seen changes of comparable scale in the historical annals. But those who argue that what we are undergoing today is unprecedented likewise make a legitimate point— changes are coming at us at an unprecedented rate. Both are correct. *How can that be?*

One helpful way to look at these technology-inflected revolutions is as historical waves: the amount of change— the *amplitude*—is comparable from one wave to another. The waves of the previous revolutions are the same size as those of the current one, thus the argument of the "this is nothing we haven't seen before" crowd. But each successive wave is compressed into shorter diachronic frames. Each revolution's waves have a higher *frequency* than the one before it. Thus the "this is unprecedented" crowd is also correct. So, while we are certainly not the first generation to witness revolutionary cultural change, we don't have the luxury of waiting four or five generations to see how things turn out.

The media tend to present future-of-work scenarios as binary, with the workforce entering either a time of historically unprecedented disruption or something much less wrenching. In Boston University economist James Bessen's words, it is the difference between "replacement and displacement."[3] Seen from a deeper perspective, however, both scenarios are correct—and not necessarily incompatible.

Scholars these days routinely—and ubiquitously—cite two studies as exemplars of the mild vs. dystopian perspectives on technology and the US workforce in the years ahead: the recent white papers from economists at McKinsey & Co. and Oxford University. The 2017 McKinsey study predicted that roughly 60 percent of jobs might see about 30 percent of their skills automated, but that technology would eliminate very few entire employment fields.[4] By contrast, the 2013 Oxford study concluded ominously that technological trends, especially in robotics and AI, are likely to eliminate fully 47 percent of American jobs.[5]

Replacement or displacement? Both, actually, depending on how far you are willing to look. A more careful reading of the studies' methodological approaches reveals that their conclusions are actually much more consonant than they appear. The McKinsey study looks out only over the coming ten-year period. And it makes the rather drastic assumption that, for the purposes of the study's parameters, there will be *zero development* in the technology sector. In other words, it predicts only the scale of workforce disruption that would happen in a decade if technology froze at its current levels. By contrast, the Oxford study embraces a broader twenty-year timeframe and assumes that current trends in technology innovation will continue.

It may well be, then, that the two studies are, at a deeper level, looking at the same future through different lenses. Just so, those who prophesy unprecedented change in the coming decades and those who assure the public that this is historically familiar territory are both potentially correct when seen from a Big History perspective.

In the past two hundred years, the United States has undergone two comparable prior transitions in which a majority of American workers shifted from one mode of production to a substantively new field. We are living through the third such.

In the early 1800s, the overwhelming majority of Americans tilled the land in an agricultural society that would have been largely familiar to their ancestors going back centuries. Over the course of about 150 years, American society then shifted to one in which the majority of workers worked in manufacturing. We can date these changes from 1817 to 1967. 1817 saw the first shovel in the ground to build the Erie Canal, which would profoundly quicken the industrialization of the Northeast. It was soon joined by railroads and burgeoning factories throughout the North. The year 1967 is a convenient bookend for this transition as the year in which the international gold crisis, according to many economic historians, marked the end of American manufacturing's global hegemony.

One of the inferences often taken from the "we've been here before" camp is a subtle suggestion that the next big shift will all go smoothly if we just sit back and let the historical processes unfold. But this first transition in America, from an agrarian to an industrial society, wasn't smooth. It was, in fact, rife with convulsive social, political, and economic contestation, despite having a century and a half to unfold.

Historians see the Erie Canal as the key force drawing places such as Rochester, New York, in a single generation, from an agricultural to a manufacturing economy, engendering massive social movements that included the Second Great Awakening religious revival, the antislavery movement, the temperance movement, and the women's rights movement. These took place in an area along the Erie Canal that would become known as the Burned-Over District, so named for the many reform movements that continually swept through like wildfires.

Many historians also view the Civil War as fundamentally driven by the inherent conflict between an agrarian South predicated on slave labor and a rapidly industrializing North predicated on free workers' labor. We might also cite labor conflicts in the industrial North during the late nineteenth and early twentieth centuries to underscore the fact that economic and workforce transitions of this scale are disruptive multidimensionally throughout society.

By 1967, a majority of Americans were engaged in manufacturing, while less than 5 percent of workers could still be found in the agricultural sector. Then a second major labor revolution transpired: a majority of American workers transitioned from a manufacturing economy to a service economy, which includes a range of services from hair stylists to pharmacists to lawyers, baristas, and yoga instructors.

This fifty-year transition, too, has been marked by conflict, in part due to the stagnation of middle-class wages and the specter of automation. The dynamics of the 2016 election cycle reveal a deep, dangerous, and growing divide among the electorate, fueled in part by these changes.

Now, two centuries after the first shovelfuls of dirt made way for the Erie Canal, we are undergoing yet another transition of comparable scale. If the longer-term Oxford study's conclusion about the automation of nearly half of our jobs is accurate, then it is reasonable to surmise that we will see a shift to yet another paradigm of employment for the majority of workers—and within less than a quarter century.

Those who say that over the past two centuries we have seen this all before are correct. We have, indeed, seen the majority of workers displaced and new jobs created for them repeatedly. But those who argue that we are facing unprecedented change are *also* correct. The timescale over which such transitions are transpiring is steadily shrinking as the pace of technological change quickens. For many workers, change is taking place well within the span of their careers. At law firms, research and discovery are almost entirely automated, reducing the need for entry-level attorneys; in journalism, most newspapers now routinely publish sports and corporate earnings stories reported and written entirely by computer algorithms; on Wall Street, low-cost, computer-driven mutual funds are revolutionizing the investment world—the *New York Times* in 2017 said the development is "putting pressure on even Wall Street's biggest money managers."[6] Actually, Wall Street firms have spent more than a decade shedding jobs in the face of automation: in 2000, they employed around 150,000 people, by one analysis. By 2013, it was down to 100,000.[7]

Smart systems will soon allow nonexperts to do much of the work of formerly expensively trained experts. In some cases, consumers themselves, aided by AI, will do the work of a professional—think TurboTax and LegalZoom. In others, AI-enhanced paraprofessionals will get the job done. In the end, say observers Richard and Daniel Susskind, the longstanding structures of traditional professions will be "dismantled," leaving most professionals to be replaced by "less expert people and high-performing systems."[8] Just as we are coming to terms with the idea of driverless cars, they say, "so too will we feel comfortable with the concept of teacherless students, doctorless patients, lawyerless clients, consultantless businesses, clergyless parishioners, and so forth."[9]

For consumers, automation will bring a golden age of consumption, even if workers don't always benefit. That's the central blessing and curse of digital technology: Just because something is cheap and abundant doesn't mean it is brought to you by an army of happy workers. The economists Erik Brynjolfsson and Andrew McAfee note, for instance, that more photos are now taken *every two minutes* than in all of the nineteenth century—yet Kodak is bankrupt.[10]

At the University of California, San Francisco pharmacy, a single robot has filled millions of prescriptions since 2010, simultaneously scanning all known drug interactions for people taking multiple medications and cutting down on prescription errors. During its phase-in period, the system filled 350,000 prescriptions with no errors, and pharmacists now talk about "chasing zero" medication errors in the long term, notes Rita Jew, the pharmacy director. She explains, "Once you've programmed the robot to do the right thing, it'll always do the same thing over and over again, without errors, unless humans introduce those errors along the way."[11]

Innovations like LegalZoom have given more people access to legal services, yet many lawyers are struggling to stay employed. In 2017, Whittier Law School in Orange County, California, announced that it was shutting its doors, due in part to sagging application rates. It represented the first time a fully accredited law school has closed—ever. And many experts say it's just the tip of the iceberg, as other law schools shrink, consolidate, and figure out other ways to cut costs. Nationwide, law schools have seen applications drop nearly 50 percent since 2005. Meanwhile, the *Los Angeles Times* in 2017 reported that California state bar passage rates had fallen to a thirty-two-year low.[12] In 2018, the American Bar Association reported, 34,339 students graduated from US law schools—down 26.6 percent from just five years earlier, when 46,776 students graduated.[13]

These consequences—perhaps unintended—call for the most proactive, imaginative, and farsighted government policies and educational models possible, to facilitate the least painful and most enlightened path forward. As we undergo profound transformations in the nature of work and the human relation to information and technology over the coming few decades, we need equally new paradigms for preparing the next generation for work and citizenship.

The core question all educators should be asking themselves today is: *What will be the key value proposition humans will bring ten or fifteen or twenty years from now to collaboratively work with increasingly intelligent artificial systems?* Our most important insights about how to educate today's students will emerge by reverse engineering from this question.

RUMPLE GOES TO SCHOOL

That afternoon, at Rumple's insistence, Bellamy gives him a tour of his old school.

As they walk the halls, Rumple notices that the walls are decorated, as in the past, with student work—but it seems somehow different. Upon closer inspection, he sees that, mixed in with the watercolor paintings and earnest, double-spaced essays, are blueprints, schematic drawings, and what look, at first blush, like business plans.

"It feels like we're in an odd mix of a school and an office," he tells Bellamy.

"Indeed," she says. "We've moved far beyond the discourse that encouraged some slight interdisciplinary learning of a few decades ago. Now we try to provide every student with at least a working familiarity—a literacy—in as many areas as possible, what we term omnidisciplinary literacy."

Rumple laughs. "I'm glad to see that education still clings to jargon."

"Undeniably," Bellamy says, blushing. "Perhaps more than ever. So, then you won't mind if I just get the jargon out of the way now: What students need from school today is not so much content fluency but, rather, omnidisciplinary content literacy, coupled with process fluency."

Recognizing Rumple's puzzled expression, Bellamy smiles, then continues: "Think about it: We humans are still pretty unique in our ability to make creative connections across apparently disparate knowledge areas. Someone designing a solar panel that unfolds on a space satellite, for instance, could recognize that they might find some useful ideas in the ancient craft of origami. Then, with the aid of AI programs, they can dive deeply into those respective areas and import innovative ideas into—pardon the pun—manifold scenarios to identify potential optimizations. That's the value of omnidisciplinary literacy. The time that is freed up by not bringing every student to content fluency can be devoted instead to imbuing them with process fluency."

Rumple peeks into a classroom window and sees the various groupings of students. "I assume by process fluency you mean teamwork, creativity, iteration, resilience, grit. Those were all buzzwords in my day."

"Yes, and other qualities that would be equally familiar to you, such as personalized learning—though now it's *actually* personalized, with highly sophisticated, predictive AI tools that tailor content directly to individual students."

"Fascinating."

"Also, we talk endlessly about communication skills. The ability to give a compelling short talk about an area of interest has become central to what we want every student to leave our halls with. Here—let's visit a classroom."

She stops before a set of massive double doors and pushes them open to reveal a large central room in which students and teachers are in various patterns of individual and small group work, each person fully engaged in their projects. Rumple immediately recognizes the productive energy in the room, but senses that, to his way of thinking, something seems out of place.

"This looks very much like a traditional classroom," he says, "but something's . . . different."

"You have a sharp eye," Bellamy says. "This class, like most, is multiage. It isn't segregated by grade, but by competence. When students are ready to move on to a new class or project, they move, no matter their age. In our secondary school, a given class might have first-years with fourth-years and even a few older students sitting in from the local community college."

"Well, I'm glad community colleges survived," Rumple says.

"Yes," says Bellamy, "but they're a bit different now. They're much more—how do I say this?—*porous* than they used to be. There's not as clear of a dividing line between high school and college. Students of all ages take classes in both institutions."

"In my day, that was called 'dual enrollment.'"

"Now it's just called 'enrollment,'" Bellamy says. "And since competence, not seat time, is the measure of success, traditional classes are also a thing of the past. The credit hour long ago became an antiquated concept, a relic of an era when educators had complete control over students' comings and goings and could dole out knowledge according to their calendar, not the students' needs."

"So, how do you know they're learning anything?"

"We test them continuously to find out what they've learned."

"So, you still give standardized tests?"

"Well, yes and no," Bellamy says. "They're tests, but they're not quite the kind you remember. For one thing, tests long ago stopped being something we had to administer with a student's full attention."

"I'm not sure what you mean."

"A true assessment is one that sniffs out what a student actually knows, right?"

"Right."

"So, if a student has to drop everything to take it, that naturally interrupts the flow of his or her learning. We've long relied on tests that naturally assess students as they're learning, usually without their even knowing it's happening."

"Amazing," Rumple says.

"More importantly, we've changed the very nature of what's taught in school."

"Oh my," says Rumple.

Without skipping a beat, Bellamy continues as she guides him through the clean white hallways: "For more than a century, as you know, we focused on preparing students for a knowledge economy, which assumed that they were going to have to acquire as much content fluency as possible before graduation. In the early days of my career, I remember, for instance, that we expected every college-bound student to reach calculus and take at least a couple years of a foreign language before graduating."

"Of course," says Rumple.

"Much of that content would never be used by most of them in their subsequent lives," she says, "but content was king back then. Colleges assumed that their students needed to be imbued with as much specialized content in their fields of study as possible, in order to have sufficient knowledge to gain expertise as engineers or doctors or lawyers."

"That's obvious," Rumple says.

She shakes her head. "Not so obvious today."

Seeing Rumple's surprised look, she continues: "All of that was predicated upon a world in which knowledge resided principally in the professional's brain. But, today, knowledge has been externalized. It resides in repositories that far outstrip any human capacity to know—and, what's more, it is all ubiquitously accessible, searchable, and synthesizable for every person on the planet, at no cost."

"Synthesizable?"

"The bots we have today can analyze and apply algorithms that mimic human analytical qualities to vast amounts of data, looking for patterns and connections that we might never identify."

"So, humans are obsolete?" Rumple asks, visibly disheartened.

"Hardly!" Bellamy says. "We're more relevant than ever. It's just that our role has shifted to what we can do best. We no longer have to prepare our students to be the principal dynamic repositories of information in their future lives; we ceded that cumbersome role to computers, just as we did with computation and other functions at which computers were faster and more adroit twenty years ago. Now we can concentrate on the uniquely human inputs, which are really higher-order values: creativity, innovation, collaboration, values, purposefulness. Think of the machine mind and the human mind as complementary partners rather than competitors—as a 'collective intelligence,' if you will."[14]

"It sounds creepy," Rumple says, recoiling a bit.

"Not at all," continues Bellamy. "You've seen too many Hollywood images of the Borg or the Terminator. It's nothing like that. No more than you were subsumed into a machine when you used a hand calculator to balance your checkbook or a smartphone to text friends—or, for that matter, when you learned to drive a car or operate a vacuum cleaner. By letting the machines do the tasks at which they are superior, we become, in a sense, a collaborative or collective intelligence that is augmented in comparison with either functioning alone. That was the lucid insight that has transformed all of education while you slept."

Rumple has to admit to himself that he's being drawn in by the possibilities, but asks, "How does this translate into pragmatic, on-the-ground school practice?"

Bellamy considers his question, then says, "Come with me."

They traverse a few hallways, climb a set of stairs, and end up in an old-fashioned photo darkroom. Rumple immediately feels at home as Bellamy proceeds to open a series of cabinet doors, looking for something. She finally pulls out an exact working replica of an old box camera and sets it atop a wooden tripod.

"A student built this," she says. "I've always loved it, not just for its obvious craftsmanship but for its metaphorical power."

"Metaphorical? It's an old box camera. My grandfather had one."

"It's a good metaphor for how we used to teach core subjects," Bellamy says. "Let's say a group of students wants to learn photography. We have the digital tools to teach them to make amazing photos that engage all their skill and creativity. We start with the problem 'How do I make a beautiful photo?' and proceed from there. We needn't go back two centuries and force them to use this primitive tool, for all its elegance. They needn't learn to keep their subjects still, ignite flash powder, and smear photoreactive chemicals on glass plates just to produce a photo. For that matter, they needn't learn how to load old-fashioned plastic Kodak film onto sprockets and develop it in a dark room. Modern digital tools long ago replaced those laborious physical processes. Studio-quality cameras are now everywhere: in our pockets, on our wrists." She taps her temple. "In our eyeglasses."

"Wait a minute," Rumple insists. "That's a shallow conception of photography! Students *need* to know about the chemical plates and the flash powder and all of that. No history of photography—no understanding of the art—is complete without a deep knowledge of that very chemical process, those exact steps. 'Content literacy' is a scam."

Bellamy smiles. "We can—and should—teach students about the history of photography, about how the first photographers made their art. We should teach them how the process affected the product. We might even give students an opportunity to make a few silver emulsion prints."

"Absolutely," says Rumple, feeling justified in his brief indulgence of righteous indignation.

Bellamy continues: "But a student who simply wants to create a beautiful photo today, in 2040, needn't use that 1840 process *every single time.*"

"Well, of course . . ." Rumple murmurs. "I mean . . ."

"It confuses the essence of photography—making beautiful pictures—with the mechanics, with the tools."[15]

"But wait," Rumple says. "Photography, like math, is essentially a technical process. The tools are important!"

"So, why focus on a narrow, antiquated set of tools? Technology has made chemical smearing optional—I'd dare say obsolete. Students who are interested in chemical smearing can still learn about that and indulge their curiosity, if they choose—they can mount a show of chemically produced photo prints, and it would be amazing. But to require every student in every photography class to submit to that process for every photo—well, that's ludicrous."

"All right," he says. "I see your point."

"An analogue might be transportation. We certainly have young equestrians today who are enriched by their love of riding and caring for horses, but we don't ask every student to make horseback riding their principal mode of travel."

"Yes," says Rumple. "I see what you mean. But tell me again how it relates to something like math?"

"We used to spend much of the school year, at all levels, ensuring that our students were proficient at calculation, that they not only understood and were comfortable with all of the steps that calculation entailed but that they were flawless calculators."

"I see where this is going," Rumple interjects.

Bellamy smiles. "We were spending an inordinate amount of effort getting our students to be able to reproduce a function that, even as far back as the 1970s, could be done by a little battery-operated machine. We were literally training our students to be *computers*. As a result, all but a tiny, patient, dedicated few ever got past the laborious calculation stage. Ironically, the patient ones were the *only* ones who eventually saw the beauty inherent in math and its many applications. And usually they were also those lucky enough to have excellent prior knowledge and parents able to pay for extra help that, in itself, was more engaging. Once that small group made it through the slog of calculation, year after year, they were rewarded with deep conceptual understanding."[16]

"Yes, well, that seems appropriate."

"It's completely backwards," Bellamy says. "Every single student should have deep conceptual understanding."

"All right, all right. I see your point," Rumple says as Bellamy puts away the camera. They walk into the hallway.

"Let's visit another classroom . . ."

2 SCHOOL COMES THROUGH, OR "HIGHER SCHOOL"

On the morning of Monday, January 15, 1821, Boston's town fathers, known as the freeholders and other inhabitants of the town of Boston, gathered at Faneuil Hall for their regular meeting. Several urgent matters crowded the docket, including street paving, snow removal, and upgrades to the town's sewers. They quickly dispatched the first two problems—a subcommittee would look into paving Water Street and the group approved a new regulation requiring that owners, tenants, and occupants of land with public walkways "shall within twenty-four hours after the falling of Snow, cause the same to be removed from the said Foot Way or Side Walk." The penalty for scofflaws, they decided, would be four dollars—about eighty-eight bucks today—with half as much added for every day snow remained.[1]

Then the committee turned to another urgent matter: schooling and a way "to render the present system of public education more nearly perfect,"[2] according to the minutes of the meeting.

Another subcommittee had already begun discussing an audacious idea for a new school, a public "seminary" that would outfit each young man—it would accept only men—for

"Active life" and "eminence in his profession, whether Mercantile or Mechanical." Until now, the group noted, parents
had to send their sons away to private academies to get that
sort of thing.

They proposed something they called the English Classical
School.

The name would have struck a dissonant chord to Bosto-
nians of the era, since by the 1820s the term "English," at least
as it applied to education, meant one thing: modern. To be
"English" was to be real-world and practical, shunning the
rarefied "classical" Greek and Latin recitations that character-
ized private prep schools, which were designed largely to train
young men for college and, by extension, the clergy, or for
a career in law, medicine, or as a schoolmaster. While many
parents would have considered it a blessing to have a minister
in the family, in postcolonial Boston, families were beginning
to understand that their sons needn't memorize Ovid, Cicero,
or Homer to get a leg up on an office clerk's job. So "English
Classical," to early nineteenth-century ears, would have had
the oxymoronic ring of "practically impractical" or "new old-
fashioned." Perhaps that was intentional, the "Peacekeeper
Missile" of its time—a postcolonial earworm that titillated as
much as it confused.

Titillation must have won out because the committee that
day voted to raise the $4,000 needed for the salaries of four
new employees: a principal, a submaster, and two "ushers,"
young female assistants who, though in most cases poorly
trained, in this instance needed a college degree to qualify.
The committee then moved on to a discussion of the town
dock and, finally, to laying a "large and expensive Common
Sewer" beneath Atkinson Street.[3]

The English Classical School opened later that year, in a
configuration that modern school reformers would surely
recognize: 102 students filed into the top floor of an existing

school, the Derne Street Grammar School on Beacon Hill, near the Massachusetts State House. The new school's principal was George Barrell Emerson, a second cousin of Ralph Waldo Emerson.[4]

Soon after the English Classical School opened its doors, its directors would do two key things: They'd create a second, companion school that admitted girls, and they'd rename the original, eventually dropping the "Classical" earworm and calling it the Boston English High School for Boys, or simply the English High School.[5]

It was the first public high school in America, and it was, at least at first, aimed at one key goal: educating young teenagers to qualify for new, high-paying, tech-focused jobs. The tech would hardly be considered cutting-edge to modern sensibilities, but, in 1821, American parents saw it for what it was: an exciting opportunity that prepared their sons for the app development, computer engineering, and cybersecurity of its age. Over the course of more than a century, the school and its countless imitators would give rise to what may be one of the most profound social shifts in modern history: the rise of mass secondary education.

But in 1821, the town fathers at Faneuil Hall were focused more narrowly, on one seemingly intractable dilemma: how to cope with a world that was shifting beneath their feet. At the time, a manufacturing, agricultural, and transportation revolution was, quite literally, building steam all around them. A communications revolution, via the telegraph, was not far behind. High school would be the next generation's training ground for the revolution.

If we want to understand what our current education system, faced with seemingly unprecedented technology-based disruption, must do now, we should understand what it did the first time around, nearly two hundred years ago. In a word, it slowly, deliberately reinvented itself, reverse engineering an entirely new parent-driven "higher" system that broadened opportunities for millions of young people.

While English High imitators appeared across the country within years, the reinvention didn't take place overnight. More than a century would pass—as well as three all-consuming wars and a Great Depression—before the typical American eighteen-year-old was a high school graduate. But the slow-motion uprising that began on the top floor of Derne Street Grammar School would change our public education system forever, making it more systematic, more purposeful, more responsive, and, eventually, more democratic.

It would also lay bare an important debate that still resonates today: Is the purpose of education to produce good workers or good citizens? Or both?

Surveying the nation's most important social mechanisms a few years ago, the renowned education scholar and activist Theodore H. Sizer called high school "the oxygen of democracy: the one place where all of our adolescents, save some unlucky or neglected ones, have a chance to rub shoulders with young people both alike and different from themselves."[6]

If America is a melting pot, high school is surely its crucible.

English High and the schools it inspired trained accountants, bookkeepers, merchants, manufacturers, stock brokers, newspaper editors, and even tech-focused farmers—"a new generation of men of affairs," one observer wrote, "who shall take into the counting-room and factory a capacity and honesty which ensure an honorable success." In the bargain, high schools also promised to save the republic, helping graduates resist the appeal of demagogues. For females, the expectations were high, but somewhat different: High schools would create "a class of women who can make pure, intelligent, refined homes out of moderate means, and altogether exalt the life of the Republic,"[7] historian William J. Reese wrote. More than a few female high school graduates would become capable teachers for a restless, westward-expanding population.

Massachusetts lawmakers had already laid the groundwork for English High with a series of laws requiring that towns build and maintain public schools. The first measure, in 1647, just a generation removed from the Mayflower landing, became known as the "old deluder" law, a reference to the fight against Satan's power to keep the illiterate from understanding scripture.[8] In 1789, state lawmakers approved a measure that required towns of 50 or more families to provide an elementary school that held classes for at least six months each year. Towns of two hundred or more families were required to provide a grammar school offering instruction in classical languages. The 1789 law was not always well enforced and the legislature provided no funding for the mandate. But many towns found that it was cheaper to simply maintain a school than to pay the pesky fines. And by 1821, families didn't need a law to tell them change was coming. As recently as 1800, an area farmer had reported that, for his sons, school wasn't necessarily a game-changer. "The Bible and figgers is all I want my boys to know," he said.[9] But the War of 1812 would serve as a kind of industrial wake-up call, cutting off America temporarily from the benefits of foreign commerce and manufacturing. New Englanders realized they couldn't rely on Europe—they had to build their own, homegrown industrial system. With technology advancing and Boston booming, families understood that something more than "the Bible and figgers" was required. Six years of basic elementary schooling simply weren't enough. Young people needed more.

The driving force behind English High was a Unitarian merchant named Samuel Adams Wells, a grandson of founding father Samuel Adams who, along with four compatriots, all of them Unitarians (two of them ministers), envisioned a new, advanced kind of "people's college," a three-year "higher school," with students selected by entrance exam from among the sons of a quickly assembling mercantile middle class. Its clientele would be Boston-area twelve-year-olds destined not for the farm or the clergy, but for new clerical and administrative jobs in big factories, accountants' offices, investment banks, railway depots, and other newfangled workplaces.

To get these new jobs, young people needed a different kind of advanced education, offering not just reading, basic math, logic, and grammar but also algebra, geometry, geography, ancient and modern history, political philosophy, composition, public speaking, and the "stile of the best English Authors, their errors and beauties."[10] Also, since this was Boston, English High second-years would get a taste of navigation and surveying.

Beyond the new job skills, Wells and his compatriots saw advanced education as a kind of basic obligation of the Enlightenment. As with shifts in technology, by the 1820s, attitudes about young people were rapidly changing. Rev. William Ellery Channing, another Boston Unitarian, had begun challenging his followers to see past traditional Calvinist beliefs about original sin. Children, he maintained, weren't simply little adults, born in sin and inherently wicked. They were highly malleable, "as pliable as fresh clay," noted historian Steven Mintz. Add to this the ascendant Romantic notion of children as symbols of "purity, spontaneity, and emotional expressiveness"[11] and the stakes for adults had never been higher. Children's well-being—and futures—depended on helping them develop good habits, self-control, and strong moral character. If adults were to raise pious, faithful offspring, they needed to guide them toward God, not beat the Devil out of them.

Simple demographics also played a role. Since the American Revolution, birth rates had been dropping. Lower birth rates meant smaller families, which focused more attention

on each child as an individual—the first childrearing manu-
als appeared during this era, as did the radical idea that children should be afforded full personhood. Mintz has noted, for
instance, that separate nurseries first appeared in middle-class
homes around the turn of the nineteenth century, and that
the high chair became a common piece of furniture, allowing
children for the first time "to sit in a position of prominence
at the family dinner table."[12]

Channing promoted what became known as "self-culture,"
maintaining that every person—or at least every boy—
deserved an education "because he is a man, not because he is
to make shoes, nails, or pins."[13] This notion would have a profound effect on educators such as Horace Mann, who took up
the cause of self-culture and fought to make schooling a more
integrated part of civic life. If schools didn't prepare children
to become good citizens, their hearts imbued with "the love
of truth and duty, and a reverence for all things sacred and
holy," he warned, "then our republic must go down to destruc-
tion, as others have gone before it; and mankind must sweep
through another vast cycle of sin and suffering."[14] School, in
other words, as a bulwark against societal decay, could literally
save America from the fate of prior city-scale republics as the
country embarked upon the first experiment in human history to forge a republican democracy built on a national scale.

Like the many high schools that would follow, English
High offered what was then considered a terminal degree.
After three years of study, students moved straight into the
workplace and, in a real sense, into adulthood, with no plans
for more formal schooling. Nearby, a few towns experimented
with different models—Plymouth in 1826 converted its Latin
Grammar School into a high school that offered "a good practical English education," as well as Greek and Latin.[15] But
what we now think of as public high school's primary role—
preparation for college—wouldn't emerge on a large scale for

at least twenty more years and, in most towns, for forty years, with the creation by Congress of the first land grant colleges in the 1860s. At most public high schools, workplace prep would predominate for decades—by some estimates, clear into the 1930s, when the Great Depression for the first time pushed more than half of young people to enroll in high school. Even the seemingly baseline idea of "high school for all" wouldn't become a reality until after World War II.[16]

What's perhaps most important—and most difficult—to understand about English High and its descendants isn't how revolutionary it was, but what a gamble it was, and what families gave up to send their children there. Throughout the nineteenth century and well into the twentieth—even during subsequent periods of technological and social change—families carefully weighed high school's costs and benefits. Sometimes they enrolled their children; most times they did not. They calculated the huge value of teens' work and, more often than not, sent them off to jobs, not to school. To the families of those 102 boys who first ascended the steps to English High in 1821, committing their twelve-year-old to "higher school" was a huge, if calculated, risk.

Slowly, families and communities began to favor the new odds. Over the next two decades, about thirty public high schools appeared throughout Massachusetts. In 1838, Philadelphia's Central High School opened, and soon educators would establish a public high school in New York City. By 1851, eighty cities had public high schools.[17] By 1860, on the cusp of the Civil War, the US boasted more than 320 public high schools.[18]

At least at first, most high schools were what we would now indelicately call "dropout factories," with the difference that our forebears dropped out to apply their education to what they perceived as compelling and lucrative job opportunities. Many students didn't stick around to graduate because the advantage gained through just a year or two of attending classes made dropping out not only sensible but, to most families, profitable. Seven years after English High opened its doors, a visiting committee from Providence noted that while it admitted from sixty to eighty boys annually, just eight to ten ever graduated, since local demand for clerks was so high.

By midcentury, historian Reese has noted, more than half of English High students dropped out before junior year. This was common elsewhere, he wrote, such as in Cleveland where Superintendent Andrew Freese in 1856 complained that only one boy in ten made it to graduation. "The boys being usually expert arithmeticians and reading penmen, are in request to fill situations in Banking Houses, Railroad Offices, Counting Rooms, etc., and more are ambitious to gain such positions than to reach the end of the course of study and graduate," he wrote, adding, "This is to be regretted."[19]

By then, public schools faced another challenge: immigration. Historian Carl Kaestle has noted that between 1840 and 1850, while the US population grew by just 35 percent, the immigrant population exploded, rising 240 percent.[20] In New York City, by 1850, foreign-born residents represented more than half of the entire population, stoking, in equal parts, prejudice and panic.[21] Once again, school was the answer: A state assembly committee advised that the only "rectifying agent" was to put these unwashed immigrants into public schools, which would "decompose and cleanse the impurities which rush into our midst."[22] This was not an entirely new idea. As early as 1836, educator Calvin Stowe, spouse of the author Harriet Beecher Stowe, had warned, "Unless we educate our immigrants, they will be our ruin."[23]

Once more, high school enrollments swelled as civic leaders openly asserted that the "moral mission" of public schools was to prevent crime and minimize the effects of poverty.[24]

Then, as the twentieth century dawned, something else happened: High school education became dramatically more widespread.

Historian Joseph Kett has called the first two decades after 1900 "the era of the adolescent" in Europe and America. As couples spaced their pregnancies more tightly, he noted, a new type of family emerged: one in which all of the children were teenagers at the same time. More significantly, he also found that in the six decades leading up to 1900, the proportion of people in America aged 45 to 64 nearly doubled. Simply put, more parents were surviving to see their children become teenagers.[25]

By 1900, the modern office—or at least the services it now provided—had become "indispensable to the managing of government, the dispensing of public utilities, the distribution of retail commodities, the production of manufactured goods, the exchange of money, and the insuring of property and life," wrote historian Sharon Hartman Strom.[26] And it developed an "insatiable demand" for high school–educated workers. As a result, high schools promoted their offerings as the way to score a coveted office job—and parents began demanding career-focused coursework for their kids.[27]

Economists Claudia Goldin and Lawrence Katz have noted that by 1920, ninety-nine years after English High opened its doors, more than one in four workers held jobs for which high school or college was expected. Between 1910 and 1940, as more office jobs became "rationalized, routinized, and subdivided," American high schools expanded at an unprecedented rate, eventually enrolling more female than male students— females would graduate at higher rates as well. The so-called high school movement would guide the US to near-universal secondary school attendance, at the time an unprecedented democratic achievement and one that many other nations considered solely a privilege of the elite. The rest of the world,

Goldin and Katz wrote, would need decades to catch up.[28] Ryan Avent, a columnist for the *Economist*, put this achievement into broad historical context, writing that humanity "spent millennia figuring out ways to augment its physical strength, through wheels and pulleys and animal-power and steam and electricity, but, in the space of just over a century (1830–1940), humanity suddenly mobilized an enormous share of its *cognitive* strength."[29]

Today, we are living with, benefitting from, and struggling with the legacy, strengths, limitations, and heightened expectations of the forms this dramatic surge in American education took in response to a previous century's industrial revolution.

In 1983, the seminal government report *A Nation at Risk* proposed that the US education system had spent the thirty-five years since the end of World War II committing "an act of unthinking, unilateral educational disarmament."[30] Two years later, the education scholars Arthur G. Powell, Eleanor Farrar, and David K. Cohen offered an anything-but-military metaphor, coining the phrase "shopping mall high school."[31]

Their analysis was oddly of its time but, thirty-five years later, it remains spot-on. By the mid-1980s, Americans had developed a hard-earned, unshakable belief that every young person should attend high school—a notion that two generations earlier would not have been a foregone conclusion—but the scholars found that in the interim something strange had happened: the schools themselves had developed a culture that implicitly valued attendance over achievement, happiness over hard work.

Like shopping malls, they wrote, high schools offered ample free parking and "something for everyone." Decades later, the shopping metaphor is rarely invoked by school reformers, but it describes the typical high school perhaps more accurately than ever. Like the mall, from the day it opens, it strives to attract and keep the largest possible crowd. The mass-produced offerings may be appealing but buying is strictly optional. Most days, just a handful of shoppers make purchases. Many come simply to window-shop, eat, drink, and spend time with friends.

Like malls, high schools offer higher- or lower-prestige versions of the same items—College Calculus to Consumer Math, AP English Literature to Basic Reading. Students and families who want more challenge can find it. Learning has its value, Powell, Farrar, and Cohen wrote, but it is "profoundly voluntary."[32] One student told them, "You can do whatever you want here . . . You can be a scholar or a total idiot."[33]

Completing one's duty to the institution, they found, comes less from mastery of subject matter than from year upon year of dutiful, orderly attendance. The phenomenon was not new and, despite what many may believe, it was by no means a product of 1960s permissiveness. Powell, Farrar, and Cohen were quick to point out that there had *never been* a "golden age" of high school—not in the 1890s, the 1930s, or the 1950s. They highlighted a survey, reaching back to 1933, that found most high schools made "strenuous efforts" to avoid failing students, especially those judged to have lower academic abilities. In more than half of schools surveyed, teachers said they promoted those who learned little. In many Depression-era high schools, progress in school was "detached from progress in learning."[34]

By the late 1950s, just as America's post–World War II industrial society was making formal education more important than ever, sociologist James Coleman found that adolescents were actually doing *less* in school, squeezing "maximum rewards for minimal effort." That was 1959, and Coleman, who would go on to transform American schooling with the so-called *Coleman Report*, had just spent two years studying the "climate of values" at several midwestern high schools. He found that sports and socializing ruled: More than 40 percent of boys told him they wanted to be remembered in school as a "star athlete," while fewer than 30 percent wanted to be known as a "brilliant student"—despite the fact that, as Coleman wryly pointed out, the American high school was "an institution explicitly designed to train students, not athletes."[35]

A decade later, researcher Philip W. Jackson would be the first to identify a "hidden curriculum" that each student (and each teacher) must master to make his or her way through school.[36] While academic demands comprised the "official" curriculum, Jackson wrote, many of school's rewards and punishments, those that seem dispensed on the basis of academic success and failure, are really more closely related to the mastery of the hidden curriculum. Then, as now, the common practice of teachers giving students credit for *trying* (as opposed to actually learning) serves as perhaps the best example of how important the "procedural expectations" of school really are—a model student, Jackson wrote, might not necessarily be a good one, but a compliant one. He also pointed out that teachers most often scold students for procedural, not academic violations: arriving late, making too much noise, disregarding directions, and so forth. "The teacher's wrath, in other words, is more frequently triggered by violations of institutional regulations and routines than by signs of his students' intellectual deficiencies," he wrote.[37]

Powell, Farrar, and Cohen would write of observing hundreds of teachers at work, finding in most cases that they displayed "no sense of intellectual purpose" aside from getting through class periods, covering necessary material, or some combination of the two.[38] They found that educators had somehow managed to create that most unlikely of places, an anti-intellectual school—one, they wrote, in which "the popular passion for education and the popular contempt for intellectual work were woven tightly together."[39] What other scholars have dubbed "classroom bargains," they called "treaties"—so much for the shopping metaphor. But they accurately described the implicit, often unconscious agreements that schools and students make: Show up each morning, don't make trouble, and we won't challenge you too much.

They found that most families—and most educators—actually felt good about this arrangement. It made a kind of perverse sense. If these institutions are judged by one key metric—graduation rates, or attendance until the final day—schools were improving all the time. If attendance stays high, the mall stays open.

Here's the larger problem: If just a few students actually achieve at a high academic level, the undereducated majority soon realize that they don't measure up. The cumulative effect is a society that supports schools as a civic and social institution but sees little value in high-quality learning.

But if students are there only to serve time, whatever happens in those four years doesn't really matter. If schools strove for *competence*, not time served, things would be different.

There is a tendency to treat received paradigms of education as fixed canons, apotheosized as inviolable fixed laws that seemingly have always been. But that, of course, is not at all how educational practice actually evolves. The progenitors of today's high school model were improvising in response to the imperatives of a particular historical moment, striving to see ahead into the needs of future decades amidst a new economic and technological landscape, entrepreneurially experimenting with innovative forms in the hopes of meeting a newly emergent set of societal challenges. None were perfect, but the experiments that best met those challenges (or, at any rate, which were perceived by contemporaries as best meeting those challenges) were scaled and elaborated, becoming paradigmatic for subsequent generations.

Exactly two hundred years after the first students entered English High, technology threatens to again shift the world under our children's feet, once more calling upon us to reverse engineer an innovative system from a new congeries of likely future scenarios. A key difference this time, though, is that time horizons have shrunk since 1821, so this act of prognosticating decades ahead, especially in an age of exponential digital growth, is fraught with unprecedented difficulty.

Repeatedly, one hears technology, business, political, and even educational leaders pronounce from the stage that we need to "revolutionize" education. This is usually accompanied by criticisms of the "industrial" model of education, of chairs in rows, of "rote" learning, though there is generally a paucity of detail about what would replace it. But decades of failed revolutions, of the "next big thing," of teaching machines and expensive technical marvels, have failed to transform a hidebound, nearly intractable system.

Revolutionizing education is neither wise nor feasible. Rather, we must *evolutionize* education, seeking to forge the optimal synthesis of the best and most germane from the received tradition with the most promising of emergent pedagogical practice. After all, the received traditions have been honed over millennia and have much that is fine and still relevant, while new educational paradigms are often faddish and ill-considered. The careful sifting and selection is essential.

This is precisely what today's more forward-thinking educators are doing, and what Jim has recently tried to do at Rocky Hill School, an independent K–12 school in Rhode Island, when he was headmaster. At Rocky Hill, Jim and his faculty pushed to implement a set of principles and practices that balance traditional and emerging skills, constantly reevaluating pedagogies rather than reifying any particular one.

What they've found is that certain traditional skills will continue to be germane to our students' success throughout their lives. Indeed, some traditional skills will take on even greater centrality in the years ahead than they had in the past, albeit in new contexts.

MAGICAL CREATURES

"Let's go over to the lab," Bellamy suggests. Minutes later, they're walking into a large space filled with interactive screens and many rows of plants and small animals in terraria.

"You have a working zoo for the biology students?" Rumple asks, nodding his approval. He is cut short when Bellamy involuntarily laughs.

Seeing his confusion and discomfort, she hastens to say, "I'm sorry—and I can definitely see why you thought this was a zoo—but it's actually our library!"

"Library? With all these plants and wildlife?"

"Look more closely," Bellamy suggests, "and tell me if you've ever seen any creatures quite like them." A bit hesitantly, Rumple steps closer to the glass, squinting to scrutinize the lifeforms, his eyes widening steadily the longer he looks.

"These are the most exotic—and beautiful—plants and animals I've ever seen! Where did they come from?"

"Our art room cum biology lab," Bellamy explains, proudly.

Gobsmacked by this revelation, Rumple stands speechlessly gawking.

"Our students bioengineered each of these as part of their design challenge to create unprecedented new and aesthetically beautiful lifeforms," she continues. "This one is my particular favorite," she says as her arm sweeps his gaze toward a frog that appears to glow with alternating color patterns. "But I'm not actually one of the judges. We'll have the final contest next week here in the library."

"I still can't believe this is the library," Rumple says in awe. "I would have thought this was the lab!"

"We are heading there, but I'm just taking a shortcut," Bellamy explains.

"But where are all the books?" Rumple asks, looking about.

"Oh, everything is digitized," explains Bellamy. "Today's library is actually a digital agora, a space in which students and teachers are encouraged to interact around good food, ideas, and the digital resources to explore any information or design thinking they could possibly wish." At this, she directs Rumple's gaze to the multiple food stations dotted around the large room, each proffering a different ethnic specialty. As his gaze is pulled away from the living art, Rumple begins to take in other sights that had escaped his attention. He notices, first of all, that there are actually many more teachers and students here than he had ever seen in this library when he was principal.

"When I ran this place," he says, "the library was often a kind of . . . ghost town."

"When it wasn't being used for detention," Bellamy adds. "I had my share of detention slips, believe me."

Rumple cringes, but Bellamy pats him gently on the back. "Come on."

They pass students sitting alone in tiny glass-enclosed stations. "These are for silent individual work," she says. Other students work in groups of various sizes, several of which include a teacher or two, interacting in casual and animated conversations. Rumple soon becomes aware that there is a steady, but slightly muted noise of people talking.

"You don't enforce quiet in the library?" he asks.

"Well, we expect a respectful, low level of noise, but we definitely encourage conversation. The library is designed to be a place for convivial interaction around ideas. If one group does get too loud, a librarian might invite them to go to a brainstorming area that is soundproofed, with walls that can be written on or turned into interactive screens."

"Now that you mention it," Rumple notes, looking about, "I haven't seen any librarians at all."

"Oh, some of them are walking about the building," Bellamy explains, moving one arm in an encompassing sweep and then pointing directly as she recognizes someone. "That's Ted, who is one of the librarians, over there, working with a group of students." Rumple turns to see a middle-aged man advising a group of students as they manipulate holographic projections of what appear to be pie charts. "Others are working remotely, since they might be helping students who are working anywhere on campus, or even anywhere in the world, on their projects. They can meet in multidimensional virtual workspaces."

"Wait a second: anywhere in the *world*?" Rumple asks.

"Travel—domestic and international—is part of the curriculum now," Bellamy says, pointing across the room to a large digital map of the world. "Each of those dots is a student working remotely."

"Amazing!"

"We long ago realized that if our students are to negotiate life in a time of swift change, the age-old practice of showing up to the same three-story brick building, in the middle of one's hometown, was antiquated and ill-advised. Travel makes their education real. It forces students to confront their deficits and rely upon their strengths."

"But travel is expensive—how do you pay for it?"

"We budget it just as we budget everything else. And we offset the costs by spending less on traditional expenses, such as a full department of teachers all teaching basic math," she says. "Because we're aiming for literacy, we can spend less on adults presiding over fluency work and more on helping students find ways to apply their learning."

"Fascinating," Rumple says.

"We also fundraise," she says. "That has not gone away. But we've retired bake sales—all that dietary fiber—what a disaster! So bad for your health."

Rumple blinks, then asks, "How do you raise money?"

"It is totally student-driven," Bellamy says. "They sell their original lifeforms, hold poetry and music nights, and—oh!" She turns to him, a twinkle in her eyes. "Can you keep a secret?"

"Of course."

"A few of our older students have created a stock-trading bot that sits in an unused office, analyzing trends in the market. They realized that we have the advantage of a super-fast web connection and the latest, fastest computers. All perfectly legal, of course, but few schools have thought of it on their own. I started them out with a $1,000 in seed money a few months ago. Since then, the bot has quietly performed billions of trades." She leans in closer to Rumple. "It has netted us a good sum of money—in fact, their parents have begun clamoring to invest with the bot."

"Remarkable!" Rumple looks around, then says a bit ruefully, "But no books."

"Well, they're kind of nowhere and everywhere at the same time," Bellamy replies, somewhat cryptically. Seeing his wrinkled brow, she quickly explains, "On the one hand, we don't shelve any physical books, the way you did here twenty years ago, but that doesn't mean there aren't books. If I remember correctly, when I was a student, we had a few thousand texts."

"Right. About six thousand."

"Well, now, every student here has immediate access to millions of books, every one of them instantly searchable and able to be compared by the 'AI-Assist' co-bot in manifold ways to query data, ideas, almost anything imaginable, from the entirety of human cultures across time and around the world."

"That's truly remarkable," Rumple concedes, "but there's something about a physical book in your hand that no digital marvel can quite duplicate."

"Many people still feel that way, too," Bellamy agrees, "which is why we try to have the best of both worlds here."

"How so?"

"Well, any faculty member or student can order an instant printing of any book or article to carry with them, manually mark up, and use like a traditional book."

"That must involve a lot of printing on paper and ink," Rumple surmises.

"Oh, we use a nanomaterial for the pages that can be instantly reused and converted into another book page for someone else when the student is done with it. Nothing is wasted, and the energy cost is minimal."

"If this is your library, I can't wait to see your labs!" Rumple says, betraying rising enthusiasm for this school of the future that had evolved while he slumbered.

"No time like the present!" Bellamy smiles, with no little sense of irony, directing him forward.

3 THE ILLUSION OF HUMANITY, OR MAYBE IT'S BEAUTIFUL

When IBM's Watson in 2011 beat the two top *Jeopardy!* champs, the typical reaction was one of awe, mixed with a measure of disbelief. Edward Feigenbaum, a Stanford University computer scientist and AI pioneer, told the *New York Times*, "Cast your mind back twenty years and who would have thought this was possible?"[1]

But the philosopher John Searle wanted to make one thing clear: the feat may have revealed ingenious programming and a huge increase in computational power, but it didn't show, as many believed, that Watson has "superior intelligence, or that it's thinking, or anything of the sort." Watson didn't understand the questions or the answers—or that some of its answers were right and some wrong, Searle wrote: "It didn't even understand that it was playing a game, nor that it won—because it doesn't understand anything."[2]

Machines are not like us, nor do they need to be. That includes machines we have grown up with over the past century. They don't work like we do or like any of the flesh-and-blood creatures they're built to emulate. "It is not necessary to understand the way birds flap their wings and how the feathers are designed in order to make a flying machine,"[3] the legendary physicist Richard Feynman wrote in 1985. Yet over the last century we've flown machines up the beach at Kitty Hawk, around the globe, into outer space and back. Airplanes—and, for that matter, space shuttles and rockets—fly differently from birds: with less agility, certainly, but with considerably greater force, speed, and endurance.

Likewise, with automobiles: To travel as fast as a cheetah, Feynman said, it's not necessary to understand the lever system in its legs; wheels will do just fine. And automobiles have left cheetahs in the dust—very much like Watson, whose brute-force computing decisively beat out human intelligence.

To create devices that can duplicate or even surpass nature's abilities, in other words, we don't need to imitate nature's behaviors. A computer does not play chess as a human grandmaster plays; while a human may pursue hunches and intuition, a computer merely crunches tens of thousands of possible positions to optimize its advantage. Yet twenty years ago, IBM's Deep Blue infamously defeated Kasparov. Was it playing chess? Does it know it won? Does it matter?

The roots of these questions date back to the very birth of AI. In 1955, the computer scientist John McCarthy, along with a group of colleagues that included John Nash and Marvin Minsky, proposed what they conceived of as a summer research project at Dartmouth. They imagined building a machine that would behave "in ways that would be called intelligent if a human were so behaving."[4] Notice that they didn't say the machine would actually *be* intelligent. That, in a way, is the point of artificial intelligence: It decouples problem solving from intelligence. "Only when this is achieved is it successful," notes Luciano Floridi, director of Oxford's Digital Ethics Lab. AI doesn't need "understanding, awareness, sensitivity, hunches, experience, or even wisdom," Floridi wrote. "In short, it is precisely when we stop trying to reproduce human intelligence that we can successfully replace it."[5] A digital machine does not have to be engineered as a direct analog to organic systems in order to accomplish similar tasks.

This will lead us down some unexpected, some would say perilous, paths. For instance, while hospitals, clinics, and university psychology departments may spend millions of dollars training thousands of human psychotherapists for intensive, one-on-one sessions that take patients from hurt to healing, a group of AI entrepreneurs has for years been exploring another way to move from Point A to Point B, focusing on what people really want from psychotherapy: emotional and psychological well-being, peace of mind, greater self-esteem, and understanding.

In 2014, Microsoft introduced a simple digital chatbot named Xiaoice (pronounced "Shao-ice") in China. It now has hundreds of millions of followers who often talk with "her" for hours, discussing loneliness, depression, job losses, and broken hearts. "It caused much more excitement than we anticipated," Microsoft's Yao Baogang said a year later.[6]

In 2016, the tech site *Mashable* suggested that Xiaoice could be in the process of passing "the biggest Turing test in history." Microsoft said Xiaoice was in a "self-learning and self-growing loop," gaining new insights from billions of conversations it has already had. "In other words," wrote journalist Lance Ulanoff, "the Turing test may not have just been broken—it could be utterly smashed."[7]

With the success of Xiaoice and similar tools, researchers have begun taking note. On its website, the company that created a virtual counselor named Woebot, a smartphone app that engages users in open-ended text message conversations, says the tool is "ready to listen, 24/7. No couches, no meds, no childhood stuff. Just strategies to improve your mood. And the occasional dorky joke."[8] A 2017 peer-reviewed study of Woebot found that it "significantly reduced" users' symptoms of depression. Researchers concluded that "conversational agents" like Woebot "appear to be a feasible, engaging, and effective way" to deliver cognitive behavioral therapy.[9]

In 2014, Michiel Rauws and Eugene Bann, two young San Francisco programmers, launched X2AI, a start-up that seeks to replicate the process of therapy using AI. Rauws came up with the idea after noticing that the conversations he was having in therapy were "often formulaic," following just a few templates and paths. He began to wonder whether AI could replicate this, or even improve upon it.[10]

The pair developed a small fleet of AI psychotherapy chatbots, among them Emma, a Dutch-language bot designed to help people with mild anxiety and fear; Nema, an English-language bot that specializes in pediatric diabetes care; and Karim, an AI counselor that has served Syrian refugees in the Za'atari camp in Jordan.[11] Rauws and Bann established a nonprofit arm to manage their philanthropic programs, which include chatbots developed to help people beset by gang violence in Brazil and HIV in Nigeria. The company stresses that the chatbots offer "help and support rather than treatment," but Lebanon's Ministry of Public Health and the United Nations World Food Program have both expressed interest in running larger pilot programs.[12]

As AI improves, humans will always be tempted to project human qualities onto it—that seems our inescapable reaction. After AlphaGo, a computer program created by Google engineers, defeated top-ranked professional Go player Lee Sedol in 2016, he apologized to reporters "for being so powerless" in the face of the tool. Then he admitted that the technology would likely "bring a new paradigm to Go." Sedol's fellow human, the European champion Fan Hui, went further. "Maybe it can show humans something we've never discovered," he said. "Maybe it's beautiful."[13]

A year later, Google debuted AlphaGo's successor, Alpha-Zero, an AI program that didn't just learn by mimicking top

Go players or relying on preprogrammed advice—it could play any two-person game, powered by an algorithm so powerful, tech writer James Somers wrote, "that you could give it the rules of humanity's richest and most studied games and, later that day, it would become the best player there has ever been."[14]

And yet: AI isn't alive. It isn't self-sustaining and it certainly doesn't respond to the world as a live creature would. "We're really closer to a smart washing machine than Terminator," said Fei-Fei Li, director of Stanford's AI Lab. "If you look at today's AI, we are really very nascent. I'm extremely excited and passionate about AI's potential, but AI is still very limited in its power."[15]

In 2013, two years after Watson reigned supreme in *Jeopardy!*, a handful of IBM scientists and chefs began teaching the device to do something decidedly more pedestrian: help out in the kitchen. They wanted to see whether a super-fast computer with access to massive data sets—mostly chemical profiles of ingredients and collections of recipes—could come up with, among other things, unexpected ingredient combinations that could spark new recipes. They set Watson free on the data and vowed to judge its "output" on three metrics: pleasantness, synergy, and surprise. Eventually it delivered, generating a large set of interesting combinations. Its first "output" was, perhaps appropriately, a dessert: a Spanish Almond Crescent featuring pepper, saffron, honey, egg, coconut milk, cocoa, lemon extract, heavy cream, and oil.

But the computer did not prepare this curious little baked good—it didn't even suggest how. Initially, Watson simply produced ingredient lists, meaningless without the inclusion of proportions—is it one egg or three?—and the strong hand of a talented chef who could interpret the output. In a 2015 cookbook based on the experiment, its creators were disarmingly modest about their work, saying Watson's output was just the jumping-off point for actual cooking. After all, they wrote, the "recipes" came from a chef "that has never tasted a single morsel of food . . . has no taste buds, no nose, nor any sensual experience of food or drink."[16]

Translation: today's computers are, in many ways, deaf, dumb, and blind. They have no idea what is happening because they have no ideas, no experiences, no connections to anything or anyone, and no awareness. Chefs had to figure out not only how to combine the ingredients but how to turn Watson's output into something that made sense on a plate.

The tech writer Mike Elgan framed the issue in a helpful way in 2018 when he posed this fraught question: *Should children be polite to Alexa?* The digital virtual assistant and its many compatriots—Google's Home and Apple's Siri among them— are becoming ubiquitous. One forecast predicts they'll be in 55 percent of homes by 2022. An eager, disembodied voice that responds to our every command and query would seem to be the perfect device to teach manners, but Elgan cautioned that this is folly. Instead, he advised, we should teach children that Alexa, for all her responsiveness and willingness to help, remains an object. Talk to her—it?—if you'd like, but remember what you're doing. "A child struggling to open a jar of peanut butter might say: 'Come on, open!'" he wrote. "Parents are unlikely to insist on a 'please' or 'thank you.' Yet that jar of peanut butter is exactly as sentient as Alexa, and has the same degree of feelings, the same amount of authority, and is deserving of the same level of respect or deference." Alexa and her kin, Elgan suggested, "do not fit in the same category as mom and dad, but in the same category as TVs and toasters."

Helping children understand that will help them stay skeptical of the devices as they grow up, he wrote. "This parental challenge is part of a much larger one: preparing kids to cope with a world of digital illusions—the fake, the phony, and the virtual. Today's toddlers will grow up in a world of deepfake videos, computer-generated Instagram personalities, holographic celebrities, and virtual reality." Preparing children for that, he wrote, means teaching them the difference between "real human people and mere machines designed to create the illusion of humanity."[17]

We must teach young people how to make sense of what computers do, and to teach them that the people are in control.

And yet . . .

A robophile might argue that we're subjecting our tech to an anthrocentric double standard. After all, we don't describe humans as blind or dumb because they can't see in infrared or make millions of computations per minute, or any number of other functions that machines readily do.

One could argue that we humans have engaged in a decades-long game of bait-and-switch with our poor digital progeny, in that each successful attainment by a machine of "intelligent" function is met by a human redefinition of what intelligence means. There was a time when a digital capacity to map complex and expansive data sets with near instantaneity, and in cogent infographics, would have been considered the domain of intellectual endeavor; once computers were capable of such renderings, however, we dismissed such capacity as beneath the real test of what makes something intelligent.

And, of course, intelligence is distinct from sentience, but here, too, we are on a slippery slope. Consciousness, as a philosophical concept, is notoriously difficult to grasp. Philosophers have argued inconclusively for centuries as to whether we can even be certain that other human beings have consciousness. How, after all, do I know that you experience self-awareness as I do? The best answer simply seems to be that the similarity and recognizability of your reactions to mine in response to certain stimuli suggests a similar state of mind. It's reasonable, then, to surmise that we are not alone in being conscious beings. (Bertrand Russell reportedly found great unintended humor in the letter he received from a self-described solipsist, who asked, "Why aren't there more of us?")

Were we to apply the same criterion to increasingly sophisticated machine minds, are we not, effectively, back to some version of the Turing test? After all, aren't philosophers really suggesting that we apply a Turing test to each other?

Another canard in this human–machine debate is to conflate intelligence with consciousness and, in turn, consciousness with sentience and with self-awareness. A careful parsing of our terms, however, suggests quite readily that these concepts could—and perhaps, for our purposes, must—be decoupled. For instance, it seems quite reasonable to suggest that machines do perform (and have for decades performed) intelligent operations regardless of any consciousness on their part. By the same token, it may be conceivable to be conscious without sentience—i.e., without "being able to perceive or feel things," as the Oxford English Dictionary defines sentience. The fact that Watson can't taste its own comestibles doesn't necessarily mean that it has no consciousness of any sort. Moreover, it seems particularly mistaken to suggest that self-awareness is a requisite of consciousness. Does an ant lack consciousness despite, in all probability, lacking self-reflection? My dog, similarly, seems singularly lacking in self-awareness, yet he surely harbors a sentient, intelligent, affective consciousness.

It is also worth noting that recent research in animal intelligence has led scientists to conclude that there is far less difference between human intelligence and that of many animals than had long been believed—that, in other words, the human intellectual advantage may be less one of *kind* than of *critical mass* that passes over an evolutionary inflection point of efficacy. Were we to apply this more broadly to include digital minds, we might posit that consciousness tends to be an emergent quality in any system of sufficient intellectual sophistication and complexity. This—or a similarly capacious—definition might free us from our anthrocentric chauvinism sufficiently to recognize that intelligent machine systems will increasingly have as much claim to consciousness in the coming decades as do biological creatures of comparable complexity, and perhaps, over time, even comparable claims to sentience and self-awareness.

Indeed, they might have more claim to these qualities in coming decades, precisely because they are products of human engineering. However intentionally or subconsciously (and both are certainly at play), humans cannot help but infuse the intelligent machine systems we build with human qualities and understandings of what constitute intelligence and consciousness. We are, in some cases with explicit intentionality and in others by mere inadvertence, applying our own understandings and reverse engineering from our own mental landscapes into mimetic machine processes.

It is quite possible that we are in the process of creating our evolutionary progeny. After all, we are ourselves insensible materials brought to chemical-based consciousness and sentience. Is it so extraordinary to suppose that we, in our age-long narcissistic endeavor of wanting to understand ourselves and to become cocreators of ourselves in the cosmos, are actually replicating nature's process in evolving us, forging a new consciousness with many human algorithms—only, perhaps, with many millions of times greater computational power? Or, if not our evolutionary successors, perhaps, at least, cognitive companions? This would not be unique even in the history of our planet; homo sapiens shared the earth—and even mated—with Neanderthals and perhaps other hominids some tens of thousands of years ago. That didn't end well for the other hominids, but perhaps our machine companions will not feel similarly compelled to extinguish the inferior fellows in their midst—or even eliminate all of their jobs.

RUMPLE'S LAB TOUR

Stepping into the adjacent building, Rumple is first met with what appears to his eyes a bewildering welter of glass-enclosed spaces on multiple levels, all clustered around a central bank of monitors at which sit several adults. In each enclosed area, variegated numbers of students and teachers are engaged in widely differing activities. After pausing briefly to take it all in, he realizes that Bellamy has walked ahead in the direction of the central monitors. He hurries to catch up.

"Clarissa, I'd like to introduce you to a very important visitor: this is Mr. Rumple, who is, um, an educational historian of sorts. Would you explain to him what's happening in the lab spaces?"

"Of course! Nice to meet you, Mr. Rumple," Clarissa says. "I'm Dean of Academics." She dives in with what appears to be her characteristic enthusiasm: "So this is where all of our classes meet for virtual interactive learning. Over there, as you can see, is a group of students who are building a model Mars base for a colony of twenty—it improves greatly on several of the current models."

"Current models?" Rumple asks. "How many are there?"

"Honestly, I've lost count," Clarissa says. "Every spring it's a new model. I can't keep up."

"Fascinating," Rumple says, astounded at the range of materials students have at their disposal. He sees them moving complicated technology that interlocks into variously configured shapes for living and working spaces and notes that each piece, oddly, has a floating display of information and data hovering in the air above it. He points this out, questioningly.

"Oh, those parts are not physically real," Clarissa explains. "They're holographic projections that are exact representations of the latest International Space Agency designs. The infographics hovering over each piece are what actual colonists would see as an augmented information overlay. The same technology can be used in almost infinite ways. For instance, over there, do you see the more traditional classroom with students talking around a seminar table?"

Rumple confirms as he sees about a dozen students gathered with two teachers around an oblong table, intent upon discussing something, though he can't help noting one student who appears a bit outlandish. "Oh, Luke prefers to use his avatar of Gandalf on some days," Clarissa explains. "He says it makes him more comfortable to project his holograph in the classroom on days when he's feeling particularly shy. In fact," she continues, "several other students that you see are actually avatars."

"The rest all look like regular kids to me," Rumple observes.

"Well, they are, but some are avatars, nonetheless," Clarissa clarifies. "The blonde girl with the blue dress on is actually named Reginald."

"Oh," nods Rumple, knowingly. "I've had many gender-fluid students."

"No, you misunderstand. Reginald is an African American boy who is running an experiment to understand how people respond to his avatars as he takes on different gender and ethnicity patterns. The blonde girl is his avatar for today. While he participates actively in his regular class via today's avatar, the algorithm he has codesigned with his AI-Assist is monitoring every detail of the behaviors among those in the class and comparing them with how they responded to his Latinx male avatar or others he has tried. To ensure a control sample," she adds with a wry smile, "he came to class one day as a ten-foot-tall dragon."

"Fascinating," Rumple says.

"Also, the four Chinese students on one side of the seminar table are not physically here," Clarissa continues. "Those are their mimetic avatars from our sister school in Beijing."

"So those students are sitting somewhere in Beijing, projecting their images into this classroom in real time?" Rumple asks.

"Maybe. I'm not exactly sure. You see, with the time zone difference, it would be about 2 a.m. in China right now. Some of those students might choose to be up in the middle of the night for synchronous participation, but they might also have set their AI-Assist avatars to participate in the discussion while they sleep; it will then summarize the discussion for them or allow them to recreate it when they're awake."

"Hmm," Rumple observes, "I see a couple of the Chinese students, at least, have contributed to the discussion just since I've been watching. Those, I guess, are the ones who are awake now in Beijing."

"Well, not necessarily," Clarissa corrects. "The AI avatar has built an extensive database of personality and intellectual traits on each student as it has interacted with them through their lives. It is able to use sophisticated predictive algorithms to anticipate what each might say in any discussion. In other words, you might be seeing a live person projected from Beijing, or their AI avatar joining the discussion but using what it understands would be their perspectives."

"Good heavens!" Rumple replies.

"Indeed," she says.

Just then Bellamy steps in. "I should mention that the Beijing students also help with fundraising. They pay tuition for the chance to get a seat at these tables. It really helps with the bottom line."

"Fascinating," he says.

"Clarissa, can you explain to Mr. Rumple what's on your monitor?"

"Of course! As you can see, these displays allow a handful of us to keep track of what's happening in every room. Here, for instance, is the display of the seminar classroom we were just observing."

Rumple can readily identify the students (avatars or otherwise) from the classroom discussion, but he is particularly struck by what looks like a vast network of webbing overlaid on the images of the students, along with floating data feeds that appear beside or above each student on the monitor. "The webs are indicators of the flow of conversation," Clarissa continues, answering Rumple's question before he asks it. "They indicate how many times a student has spoken, in response to what prompt, and directed to whom. We can mine these data from one classroom session or aggregate them across an entire year in many and deep ways. This is not to enforce any particular behavior or participation, necessarily, but just to more richly inform our teaching and individuation to each student and to the collaborative dynamic of the whole class. The data can be set to indicate—in real time—any of about 10,000 qualities I might be monitoring, be it social discomfort or attentiveness. Incidentally, this is also available in real time to the teachers in the seminar from their seats at the table—on monitors that can't be read by those sitting next to them. This helps them to continually adjust the dynamic in an informed way throughout the discussions."

"So, you control all the classrooms from here?" Rumple asks.

Clarissa shoots Bellamy a silent look. "We don't like the word 'control' at all," she says. "From here, we can monitor the flow of the classrooms and the students' learning. We can even voice over or interject ourselves as avatars from here into any of the classrooms to guide, make suggestions, or encourage the students. We obviously don't tend to do that in classrooms with teachers, but we do so with some regularity in the classes where students are self-directing a design challenge or others are independently pursuing project learning."

Rumple suddenly notices with alarm that one of the monitors displays a video image of several students sampling boiling red lava flows atop the cone of an active volcano. "My goodness!" he exclaims. "Where are they? That looks like a very dangerous field trip!"

"No need to worry," Bellamy laughs. "They're right over here, safe and sound."

Rumple looks to see the very students from the video feed—they're wearing headsets and walking gingerly around an empty room, occasionally bending as if to pick up a sample. "The monitor allows us to see the XR environment they inhabit via their headsets," Clarissa explains. "Here," she suggests, "let's join that class—over there. They're taking a field trip to Paris today."

Rumple is directed first to view another largely empty classroom in which several students and a teacher are sitting in clusters around tables, each with a paper cup at his or her place—and then to the monitor, where he sees them sitting at the same-sized tables in a classic Parisian café, replete with delicate ceramic coffee cups and the Eiffel Tower as background. Clarissa holds three headsets and extends one to Rumple.

As soon as he places it over his head, Rumple is transported to the Parisian café. Beside him, both Clarissa and Bellamy pop into the scene as they don their headsets. At each table, a virtual waiter is taking the students' lunch orders.

Rumple, who speaks French fluently, quickly realizes that he can hear the avatar waiters speaking in French, but that he hears softly yet distinctly in his ear a simultaneous, flawless English translation each time one of them speaks. After the waiters leave, vigorous conversations ensue among the students at their respective tables. Clarissa points out to Rumple that each table is seeded with AI-generated avatars of French students who are explaining French culture and cuisine. Indeed, Rumple notices that he is receiving the same real-time English translation in his ear whenever the French students speak. The translations shift to different students as his attention shifts from one to another.

After observing for a few minutes, the three of them remove their headsets and find themselves again at the central monitors. After catching his bearings, Rumple says, "That was remarkable! But how are your students expected to learn French if they always hear everything in English translation?"

Clarissa involuntarily shoots Bellamy a confused look. "I should have explained," Bellamy tells her. "Our guest has been, well, out of the loop for a while." Turning to Rumple, she adds, "We no longer teach foreign languages as a regular subject."

"What?"

"When the AI universal translators became so effective several years ago, it no longer seemed to make sense to expend so much school time and resources teaching students a foreign language, when, for all intents and purposes, they were never going to use it in their personal or business lives."

"In its place," Clarissa adds, "we require every second-year student to take a yearlong course teaching them how to be culturally informed, respectful, and effective visitors to other countries, whether doing business there or just as tourists. It also teaches about the history of each place. That's the class we just joined. Next week, they'll be in Seoul."

Rumple, who recalls that he had enjoyed learning French as a young man, can't help feeling a bit resistant to this change. "But they lose so much by not learning a foreign language!" he protests.

"No doubt," agrees Bellamy. "I, myself, speak four languages and feel that learning those has given me a more nuanced feel for those respective cultures. But there just isn't time for everything in the curriculum, and, as one traditional skill becomes less essential to success or citizenship, it tends to be replaced by another. This has happened throughout the history of education."

Rumple concedes, "That's true. There was a time when every educated person was expected to know Latin and be versed in classical antiquity, but that was relegated to the margins in the twentieth century."

"Just so," Bellamy nods. "In fact, it was the parents, many of whom travel for both work and play, who pushed hardest for us to transform our foreign language requirements to a more focused global citizenship curriculum. They felt we were spending too much time and departmental resources on skills that would rarely if ever be used in the age of universal translators. They were upset that we were taking too much time away from the skills that matter most today, such as computational and big-data thinking."

"But, earlier, you said that you continue to consider it an important broadening experience for students to travel," Rumple protests one last time, with perhaps diminished conviction, as he anticipates Bellamy's answer.

"Absolutely, travel is an immensely broadening experience that we wish for every student," she replies, "but traveling is not the same as speaking a foreign language. Besides," she adds, "students who are in Paris today and Seoul next week, then perhaps Beijing the following month, would have to know French, Korean, and Mandarin if they didn't have access to universal translators."

Clarissa, sensing Rumple's discomfort, is quick to add, "We do have some students who simply love to learn foreign languages—and they're able to pursue their passion with electives. They can, for instance, return to the Parisian café any time they like to practice conversational French—we simply turn off the simultaneous translation."

Rumple stands back to take in the full scope of the panoply of labs with active, engaged students learning everywhere about him. "Well, I must admit," he says aloud, "this is a veritable hive of enthusiastic, experiential learning. I find myself thinking that Dewey would be very happy in this environment. The AI XR technology has allowed you to create infinitely malleable constructivist learning environments, individualized to each student."

Beaming with pride, Bellamy rejoins, "Indeed." Taking his arm, she adds, "Come, let me show you how one of our students is crowdsourcing her design project with over ten thousand students from around the globe."

4 THE TRUST MACHINE

Our parents were as different as stars in the sky, but as we grew up they couldn't have been clearer—more unambiguous, more unyielding—about one key truth: *Strangers are dangerous.*

As a result, their rules were simple:

Don't talk to strangers.

Don't get into strangers' cars.

Don't go into strangers' houses.

Who could argue? Centuries—perhaps millennia—of social conditioning had made these ideas so patently obvious (one can imagine eighteenth-century parents warning: *"Don't get into strangers' carriages."*) that we never questioned them. As we got older, we made all manner of horrible decisions and took all kinds of stupid risks. But even the most reckless among us knew that if we wanted to survive into adulthood, we'd better not consort with strangers.

Then we all got mobile phones and none of that mattered.

In the course of a few years, it seemed, centuries of social conditioning evaporated. We now talk to strangers constantly, routinely, via social media and dating apps. Despite bringing no familial, cultural, or geographic connections to many of these interactions, we fight and commiserate with these strange people, listen to their stories and rally around them when they're attacked. We raise money for their causes, offer heartfelt advice, and spend hours working to persuade them of the rightness of our political views. We follow, like, and friend them. On occasion we swipe right, then date, court, and marry these strangers.

We get into strangers' cars all the time—often in strange cities and, more improbably, in foreign countries where we do not speak the language. Ride-sharing apps have turned this patently risky behavior into a yawn. The only question, for most of us, is whether we're feeling brave enough to ask the stranger whose car we've just climbed into to turn down the music—or, if we're really feeling confident, to ask him to take a faster route. Before we even climb into the stranger's car, we're confronted with a related question: Would we like to bring down the cost of this encounter by sharing the back seat *with more strangers*?

Getting into strangers' cars has become not just an acceptable idea—it's such a good and sustainable and profitable idea that thousands of people, most of them as smart and well raised as we are, now work full time to help us do it more cheaply and efficiently. They fight for the privilege of being the best get-into-strangers'-cars app in the world. In fact, many of the more principled among us angrily boycotted the biggest of these companies a few years ago, when it demonstrated insufficient moral character in its boardroom. We were glad, then, to have a choice of ways to search for strangers' cars.

Most improbably, we go into strangers' houses. We smell their flowers, pet their cats, admire their family photos, poke through their refrigerators, enjoy their hot showers, take their books off the shelf, and, unbelievably, sleep in their beds. We sleep well. In the morning, we share a cup of coffee, ask for directions, and get a primer on the best neighborhood restaurants.

With a few notable exceptions, it turns out, the strangers are not so dangerous.

At the same time, another unexpected behavior is taking shape: We're losing trust in our old, reliable institutions, the ones that have long formed the basis of our social foundations. When the Gallup Organization in 2018 asked Americans which of fifteen key institutions we trusted "a great deal" or "quite a lot," it found that most of us trust not ten or twelve or even half a dozen. We trust just three: the military, small businesses, and the police. Fewer than half of us trust the remaining ones quite as highly. This dirty dozen includes essentially every institution we grew up with and have always implicitly trusted: our churches, public schools, doctors and nurses, Congress, the US Supreme Court, and our local newspapers. Fewer than one-third of us now trust banks.[1]

Yet we sleep in strangers' houses.

What is happening here?

We have, in a sense, transferred a large portion of our precious trust out of the real world and into the virtual, the digital, or at least to a version of the real world that is easily mediated by these. Somehow, after handing over a credit card and password—the same weak password we use just about everywhere else online—we now implicitly believe that what our iPhone tells us about the world is real and true and trustworthy—more real than what our parents, our coworkers, our pastors, and our community leaders tell us. Our phone—and the *phone* function, of course, is the oldest, least interesting feature—has become more reliable than our flesh-and-blood human connections, more reliable than most of the old familiar things we've always relied upon.

Anyone who follows technology closely shouldn't be surprised. Digital tech has always promised to reshape our realities—as did the telephone, even when it was a bulky, crank-operated device built into a wooden box on a drug store wall. It is probably worth thinking about the telephone for just a minute here, because its history can help illuminate a larger reality.

The telephone began life more than a century ago, as one of several "space-transcending" technologies—they included the automobile and the radio—that expanded the geographic scope of users' lives and, in the process, shifted the bases of social solidarity "from bloodline and place to occupation and taste,"[2] wrote the sociologist Claude S. Fischer. That seminal trio—the telephone, the automobile, and the radio—freed us from the limiting constraints of our families and our neighborhoods and gave us access to everything else, on our terms.

But even as inventions like the telephone offered a bigger world, perhaps more importantly they offered a promise of safety—much as a new mobile phone does for parents today as they're trying to persuade themselves that their thirteen-year-old daughter needs one to stay "connected" all the time.

This is a very old idea. A 1905 ad for home phone service in Philadelphia crowed, "The modern woman finds emergencies robbed of their terror by the telephone. She knows she can summon her physician, or if need be, call the police or fire department in less time than it ordinarily takes to ring for a servant."[3] Twenty-five years later, the Illinois Telephone Association casually suggested to rural families that they could either get a home phone or be robbed and killed: "A telephone on a farm is the greatest obstacle to rural thieves," one 1930s ad read. "A telephone can head off the theft of your chickens, hogs, harness, and gasoline—and warn folks down the road of the crooked peddler and the vicious tramp."[4]

Well, maybe strangers are dangerous after all.

Vicious tramps aside, the point remains: the telephone is—and always has been—*a trust machine*. The moment we trust it is the moment we begin to let it guide our choices and behavior. The shift from hand crank to iPhone may have taken more than a century, but the distance is very short between an ailing turn-of-the-century Philadelphia matron dialing up her doctor—or, more likely, having her servant do it—and a modern-day traveler getting off a plane in Geneva, Switzerland, walking to the curb, pressing a piece of magic glass, and climbing into a stranger's waiting minivan. In both cases, the user implicitly trusts that the system lurking beneath the surface of this strange, miraculous device will give her what she wants: it will both expand her world and, in the bargain, keep her safe.

Let's stay in Geneva for just a moment and stick with this metaphor, and our hypothetical traveler. Imagine that the minivan in question pulls up at the airport curb one recent evening. Our traveler, seeing that its license plate matches the one on her iPhone screen, slips the phone into her pocket, picks up her bag and eagerly approaches the van. She has done this a thousand times and the rides are nearly always an adventure. On occasion she has had to ask the driver to turn down the music, but that's a small price to pay. Ride-sharing is awesome, Geneva is awesome. She'll get to practice her French with the driver—she'll tip him extra, she thinks, if he doesn't criticize her terrible accent.

The van's doors slide open and what greets our traveler is indeed strange: a passenger sits at the rear of the van, her face tipped downward and illuminated by a smartphone screen. The backseat passenger looks up, sees our traveler, and offers a friendly little wave. But something is amiss. No one is behind the wheel. The minivan is driven not by a human but by a computer, or more accurately, by an advanced GPS- and infrared camera–guided machine learning system.

Our traveler freezes, unsure of what to do. She steps back, pulls out her phone—it comes alive upon recognizing her face—and double-checks the tags. The minivan exactly matches what she has ordered, but she was sure it'd be driven

by . . . a human. She has heard about these self-driving vehi-
cles rolling out across Europe, but she hadn't realized they
were so far along—or that they were being used so widely. And
she hadn't considered, really, whether she was ready to ride in
one. She hadn't planned on this.

Our traveler begins to perspire as she considers the long
ride into the city and the prospect of barreling down the E62
at high speeds with no one behind the wheel.

"Are you getting in?" the backseat passenger asks in heavily
accented English.

"I'm . . ."

"It's OK. I do this all the time. It's fine!" She waves our
traveler inside. "Come on, these things are safer than human
drivers—and they don't stare at you!"

Our traveler apologizes for keeping the passenger waiting.
She notices that another vehicle, also driverless, has pulled up
alongside the first and is now executing a perfect parallel parking maneuver, ending just inches from the van's front bum-
per. *Have all the drivers been replaced?* she wonders.

Our traveler takes one more look at the empty driver's seat,
then stares down her phone and presses the "Cancel Ride"
button. The stranger waves goodbye (with a bit of an eye roll)
as the doors slide shut to the tune of a slow rhythmic beep.
"I'm sorry!" our traveler calls as the doors click shut. The passenger goes back to her glowing screen and the van maneuvers
deftly around its parked companion, waits for three speeding
taxis to whiz by, then accelerates into the night.

The difference between our Geneva traveler and our backseat passenger—indeed, the only difference, for our purposes—is trust. Both trust the system enough to bring the
strange minivan around, but our traveler balks at the prospect
of trusting the bots to drive, despite the fact that, let's face
it, her fellow humans are pretty dangerous drivers. They kill
more than one million of their own species worldwide each

year, making car crashes the leading cause of death for children and young adults.[5] Even if robot drivers staged a *Mad Max* moto-apocalypse and set out to kill half a million people per annum, they'd still cut the traffic death rate in half.

The big question about technology has never been, and never will be, *What can it do?* Eventually, we can agree, robots and AI and smart systems will be able to do nearly everything we ask of them, more cheaply, expertly, and efficiently. The question is: *What do we trust all these systems to do?* The moment we trust them, that's the moment their labor becomes a natural, unremarkable part of our lives. We're the backseat passenger staring at our cell phone, swiping right on Tinder while the driverless minivan barrels at high speeds down the highway, toward a Geneva Airbnb we booked online.

Over the next few years, we'll be in a near-constant state of asking ourselves: *What do I trust technology to do?*

Brew me a hazelnut latte? Check.

Prepare my dinner without poisoning me? Affirmative.

Clean my apartment? Absolutely.

Grade a hundred and fifty student essays? Yes, please.

Do my taxes or find me a new mortgage? OK

Accurately fill my insulin prescription? Umm, sure, if it's accurate.

Walk my dog? Perhaps.

Design a vibrant, livable city? Well, no, not really. I mean . . .

Compose a dazzling opera, complete with libretto? Wait a minute, what?

Mete out justice in a fair, humane manner? Hard no!

Care for my elderly mother or inform me that I have cancer? Absolutely not!

We trust people with these more fraught, unpredictable, high-stakes tasks, not because the machines can't do them but because we don't *want* the machines to do them. We reserve that right for our fellow humans. Despite their relatively lousy

record—on driving, on designing cities, or meting out justice—we trust humans.

So, if we want to help our young people thrive in a world
of miraculous technology, we must forget the nouns—the AI
and robots and intelligent systems—for these will always be
changing. We must focus instead on the verbs: What it is we
trust our young people to *do* that we don't trust technology to
do? And how can we prepare them for this future?

For starters, let's not give them robots' work. Let's trust
them to do better, harder, more rigorous, more interdisciplinary, high-stakes work—and not just for the 10 percent, but for
everyone. We must expect more of young people, not only
because the world will expect it of them but because they are
begging us to do so.

For so many students, school is simply not demanding
enough—and the dilemma, of course, doesn't begin in high
school. When the Education Trust, a civil rights group that
advocates for low-income and minority students, examined
more than 1,800 math assignments given to middle school
students in six urban, suburban, and rural school districts in
2018, it found that most of the assignments featured "low
cognitive demand," overemphasized procedural skills and fluency, and provided little opportunity for students to communicate their mathematical thinking. The problem was often
worse in high-poverty schools.[6]

Similarly, when the New Teacher Project in 2018 observed
nearly 1,000 high school lessons, it found that students met
the demands of their assignments 71 percent of the time, yet
demonstrated mastery of grade-level standards on assignments just 17 percent of the time. Students spent more than
500 hours per school year on assignments that weren't appropriate for their grade and with instruction "that didn't ask
enough of them." Researchers concluded that students spent
the equivalent of six months of wasted class time in each core

subject. Overall, they found, students' school days lacked four key necessities: grade-appropriate assignments, strong instruction, deep engagement, and teachers who hold high expectations.[7]

Recent surveys show that, perhaps as a result of these dilemmas, few high school students take school seriously. As far back as 2012, the Gallup Organization surveyed nearly 500,000 students in public schools in thirty-seven states and found that while nearly eight in ten elementary-aged students were engaged in the enterprise of school, by high school only four in ten said the same. "Our educational system sends students and our country's future over the school cliff every year," researchers concluded.[8]

Other surveys have found that just 41 percent of high school students say they go to school because of what they learn in class. Of those who have considered dropping out, 42 percent say it is because they didn't see the value in the work they were asked to do.

Even as they grow more alienated from school as an institution, each day they place more and more trust in the magic devices in their pockets. They're attached to their phones because, as users, they've been trained to trust what's on the other end. On social media, their friends are who they say they are. After babysitting, the $40 that show up in their Venmo account are real. When they call an Uber or Lyft after drinking too much at a party, the face that appears onscreen is that of the person who will safely take them home.

That promise should be redeemable at school as well. Schools should be trust machines, too.

Despite their outward appearance, young people want badly for school to work—82 percent say they welcome the opportunity to be creative at school, and 65 percent—nearly two-thirds of students—say they would prefer classroom discussions "in which there are no clear answers."[9]

If we expect more, we must give them more: more autonomy and more support.

Researchers Elena Silva and Taylor White have noted that the brains of young people at around age fourteen—the age when most are high school freshmen (sorry: first-years)—are changing profoundly, their plasticity mirroring that of infants' and toddlers' brains. The adolescent brain, they write, "craves new and different experiences and easily picks up new skills and interests." At the same time, the part of the brain that controls decision making and risk assessment is still developing: "Like a toddler climbing on furniture, the teen needs the perfect blend of independence and support."[10]

High schools that work, they say, connect students to the outside world, offer a rigorous curriculum and integrate applied and academic learning. But they also offer students structured relationships, with strong leaders and good teachers who see the need for both autonomy and support, for experiences that are both expansive and safe. At the center of these experiences is a sense of trust that adults will stick with them, guiding them as they venture into the unknown.

As it is, they wrote, most adolescents are actually cut off more than ever from adult society, forming what the sociologist James Coleman called their own "adolescent society"—despite decades of research showing that they need "consistent, intensive support from adults in the system and the community, at least every week, and often every day." Most students, they found, have "no structured supports for learning outside of the classroom" and few chances to develop "authentic, positive relationships" with adults.

More broadly, most school policies have actually diminished trust between students, teachers, parents, and administrators, driving a wedge between Americans and their schools. Researchers Anthony Bryk and Barbara Schneider have noted, for instance, that decades of federal, state, and local policies aimed at promoting desegregation—surely a noble goal—have had the unintended effect of distancing schools from the communities they serve. Surveying Chicago elementary schools in the mid-1990s, they found that nearly 30 percent of students no longer attended a neighborhood school; at the high school level, the figure was 50 percent. The "massive redistribution" of faculty resulting from court-ordered desegregation had, in effect, severed the ties of thousands of teachers to local families, Bryk and Schneider found. "A residue of social distance has been left in its wake which is now normative in many school communities," they wrote. "As a consequence, the social misalignments documented between urban school professionals and poor parents have been further exacerbated. Many urban schoolteachers have only weak ties at best to parents and the school community."

By contrast, they found that Catholic schools, particularly urban Catholic schools, function so effectively in part because they create deep bonds of trust between teachers, students, and parents, what they call a "structure of moral commitments and mutual obligations" that has a profound impact on teachers' work and students' sense of engagement.[11]

In his 2012 book *Why School?*, educator Will Richardson called our technological era a "moment of abundance" that makes real-life, inquiry-based learning both easier and more important. Schools, he wrote, must prepare students to be learners who can "successfully wield the abundance at their fingertips."[12]

As if channeling the affordances of Uber and Airbnb, which were then just finding their first customers, Richardson in 2012 actually suggested *talking to strangers* as an educational strategy. "Remember, in this moment of abundance," he wrote, "teachers are everywhere. . . . The reality is that the kids in our schools will interact and learn with strangers online on a regular basis throughout their lives. I'd go so far as to say that

I want my own kids to be found by strangers on the Internet. (I'll let that hang there for a moment.) Certainly, I want them to be found by the right strangers, the ones who share their passions and want to learn with them. And I want them to be able to discern between good and bad strangers." He added, "If you forced me to eliminate all the strangers from my learning life, people I interact with on a regular basis, I seriously don't know what I'd do. Just learn with people I know? Take night classes?"[13]

Richardson has challenged schools to ensure that students not only learn from strangers but share their work with the world. He asks: "How can you make sure that every student who walks on graduation day is well Googled by his or her full name?"

If we look around, he and others say, we'll find teachers—and classrooms—everywhere. Including in the next desk: At King Middle School in Portland, Maine, technology teacher Gus Goodwin routinely tells students that they've got to trust, rely on, and teach one another to make the classroom come alive.

"There is only one of me," he tells them. "You need to look to each other."[14]

RUMPLE LEARNS CROWDSOURCING

Bellamy leads Rumple to a room where a student and teacher are staring with singular focus at a floating hologram. It appears to be the schematic of a box, with animation of some kind of fluid or gas flowing through multiple components. The two are so engaged in analyzing the projection that they don't at first notice the visitors who have stepped into the room. Quickly after entering, Rumple also realizes that the student is talking aloud about design aspects of the contraption and that other voices are joining in the discussion; each time a distant participant speaks, her or his face pops up on monitors embedded in a wall.

Bellamy catches the teacher's attention and beckons him over to them. In a low tone, she says, "I don't want to interrupt Amanda's discussion, Bob, but I'd like to introduce you to a distinguished visitor, Mr. Rumple. Can you explain briefly what you're helping Amanda work on for her senior portfolio project?"

"Of course," Bob says, smiling. "Nice to meet you. Amanda has chosen for her senior capstone to design a more effective, lower-cost, and more easily assembled small-scale water desalination cube that is easily portable and can provide water for up to four families. They're making tremendous progress."

"Fresh water is a severe problem in the world today, far more acutely than twenty years ago," Bellamy explains.

Rumple's attention, however, has been caught by something else in Bob's comment. "You said 'they' are making progress. Did you mean the others I see on the screens?"

"Well, yes," Bob replies, a bit confused by the naivete of the question. "This is principally Amanda's project, of course, but she has over 10,000 coengineering collaborators from twenty-one countries actively participating, and, last we checked, over 50,000 people who have at least logged into the site."

Shooting Bob a mute plea for patience with their visitor, Bellamy adds, "We teach our students to crowdsource most of their larger, more complex and important projects from the third grade on. Being able to manage thousands of contributors and cull the best ideas from them while maintaining control over the project's vision and outcome is a set of skills we place great value on—not to mention that those skills are highly prized in the global business community, where so many new products and services are the result of precisely this process."

"So, Amanda is working with thousands of students around the world to build a better portable contraption to make fresh water?" Rumple says admiringly.

"Yes, but not only students," Bob clarifies. "To fulfill the course requirement for professional input, Amanda has enlisted working chemists and physicists—they've been incredibly helpful in suggesting new nanomaterials that are more effective—as well as some NGO directors who have helped her understand certain needs for portability and adoption in the neediest villages. She has also enlisted an expert from the World Bank who is helping her with her business model and scalability."

"I actually once heard one of my talented teachers joke to a colleague that students should never submit their own work," Bellamy interjoins, with a wink to Bob.

Bob, recognizing himself in the reference, clarifies, "Well, I meant it as an exaggeration, of course, because this is really Amanda's project, under her leadership. But the point I was making was that it's so different today from when I was in high school, where we were all expected to 'do our own work,' except for the rare team project."

"This is amazing," Rumple confirms enthusiastically, "but it seems an overwhelming undertaking for a high school student to organize this and then to deal with all the input from so many people!"

"Well, it is a lot of work," Bob agrees. "Our seniors work incredibly hard on these projects, and Amanda is a particular star. But we prepare all the students throughout lower, middle, and upper school to be able to pull this together in their senior year. And we give them lots of faculty support."

"Remarkable," Rumple replies.

"There are also different ways students curate the sheer enormity of input," Bellamy adds. "For instance, the design you see in that hologram represents this very well. Could you explain a bit for us, Bob?"

"Sure. After Amanda produced an initial design for what she thought might do the trick, we put her draft online for a week so that others could tinker with it at any time, 24/7. As you might imagine, we received many thousands of tweaks. An early stage of the year-long project, though, is for our seniors to build, with their AI-Assist, an algorithm to query and synthesize just such inputs."

Seeing Rumple's confusion, Bellamy quickly interjects: "For instance, Amanda worked with her AI-Assist to build a program that takes all those thousands of design tweaks over the past week, selects what appear to be the most promising, tests them in various combinations and configurations for optimal effectiveness, and suggests the new design draft that best fits all of her criteria."

"That's the design you see before you here," Bob adds. "You might have noticed, off to the side here, these data points beside the hologram; those show how much more effective the new design is compared to the previous prototype along various axes that correlate to the criteria for selection Amanda established. Now, Amanda is inviting anyone who wants to join for a live discussion of the merits and weaknesses of the resulting redesign." Pausing, he then adds by way of after-thought, "This process will go through multiple further itera-tions, of course."

"Wow!" Rumple is rendered speechless in amazement. Col-lecting himself, he asks, "And what will be the final result of all this?"

"Well, at the end of her senior spring term, Amanda will give a fifteen-minute presentation of her results," Bellamy says. "In an age of ubiquitous connectivity, we've come to see that core skills must include not only the grit and resilience to see a complex project like this through to completion but also the capacity to give a compelling short oral presentation conveying your content mastery in an accessible way to a gen-eral audience. And to be charismatic and convincing in the process."

"All of our seniors have an audience for their capstone pre-sentation that includes relevant professionals—and perhaps even some potential investors," Bob says. "Amanda's project is already generating great excitement on social media—we'll probably have to limit access for audience participation to selected VCs and NGOs."

"I'm just trying to take this all in," Rumple says to Bellamy as they step out of the classroom. "You've developed a model of highly individualized project-based learning that instills in students the skills to organize a global hive of cognitive collectivity that they then use, via computational thinking with their AI-Assist, to coordinate a progressive design refinement, culminating in an engineered proposition to solve real-world challenges. And then they present it effectively to a live global audience of experts and investors."

"Precisely," Bellamy concurs, with unmistakable pride. "Not to mention the omnidisciplinary nature of the learning and the importance we place now on building students' public speaking skills."

"It's a far cry from the public speaking students did when I was principal," Rumple says. "Compared to this, that seems positively Stone Age."

"We have made a bit of progress since you last walked these halls," Bellamy says. "Come on, there's more to see."

5   CENTAURS IN THE NEWSROOM AND IN THE CLASSROOM

IN THE NEWSROOM

Near the beginning of his journalism career, from 1998 to 2002, Greg spent four years at the Associated Press, first in its small bureau in Baltimore, then in Washington, DC. While Baltimore and other bureaus were—and are—seven-days-a-week operations, in those days a single "newsman" or "newswoman" could run an entire bureau on weekends.

At around four or five in the afternoon most Saturdays and Sundays, the bureau's fax machine—by then already rarely used—would come alive, issuing a series of single-page dispatches. Along with the weather report and the results of the Pick-3 and Pick-4 lotteries, these faxes represented some of the most consequential bits of news to emerge from AP bureaus.

On the grainy black-and-white printouts were the box scores of minor-league baseball games from around the region, cryptic little charts that laid out the results of each game. It was the reporter's job to stare at each page and write a five-paragraph story, telling the world what had just happened. During the week, this was typically the job of the AP's real-live

sportswriters, but on the weekends it fell to any warm body
unlucky enough to be on duty.

To an AP newcomer, this was, at first, an interesting logical
challenge, a sort of journo-linguistic jigsaw puzzle, with a solution that would soon appear in the back pages of the nation's
sports sections. But after the first two or three, it quickly grew
into a tedious, formulaic job. And the faxes kept coming.

More than twenty years later, the AP still produces these
dutiful little dispatches, thousands and thousands of them—
more than ever, actually. And they look exactly as they did in
1998. Here's a recent example in its entirety:

BOWIE, Md. (AP)—Noel Cuevas hit a walk-off single with two outs in
the 12th inning, as the Hartford Yard Goats topped the Bowie Baysox
4–3 on Tuesday.

Rosell Herrera scored the game-winning run after he hit a single
with two outs.

Garabez Rosa hit an RBI double and then scored on a single by
Chance Sisco in the first to give the Baysox a 2–0 lead. The Yard Goats
came back to take a 3–2 lead in the seventh inning when Dillon
Thomas hit an RBI single, driving in Juan Ciriaco.

Bowie tied the game 3–3 in the eighth when Drew Dosch hit a solo
home run.

Hartford starter Carlos Hernandez went six innings, allowing two
runs and 11 hits while striking out three. Jerry Vasto (4–2) got the win
with a scoreless inning in relief while Tanner Scott (1–2) took the loss
in the Eastern League game.

In the losing effort, Bowie got contributions throughout its order,
as five players had at least a pair of hits. Dosch homered and singled
twice. The Baysox left some scoring opportunities on the table, strand-
ing 14 baserunners in the loss.

Hartford improved to 8–2 against Bowie this season.[1]

What you can probably guess by now, given the subject
of this book, is that this story was written not by a human
but by a piece of software. Since 2016, the AP has outsourced

virtually all its routine minor league coverage to a Durham, North Carolina–based start-up called Automated Insights. A computer merges an existing database (how many games have the Yard Goats won/lost in previous Baysox matchups?) with the just-produced results of each game. Then it composes a handful of past-tense declarative sentences that lay out a basic baseball narrative. While a weary human might require the better part of an hour to steel his or her spine and produce this useful little recap, the computer composes it in seconds.

A disclaimer at the end of each dispatch tells the reader that the author isn't actually a person—and that the piece wasn't actually written as much as extruded: *This story was generated by Automated Insights (http://www.automatedinsights.com) using data from and in cooperation with MLB Advanced Media and Minor League Baseball (http://www.milb.com).*

If this is the robot apocalypse, it can't come soon enough.

Pick virtually any white-collar industry and you will find a similar story of automation tugging at its heels. The task-level changes taking place in our respective industries are just beginning to make themselves known, but we thought it would be instructive to take a look at two of them, with an eye toward what they say about work more broadly. In both industries, automation is imitating and, in most cases, improving upon, human effort, yet it is almost always supplementing and not supplanting humans. In both cases, the path forward seems equally promising and challenging, suggesting that traditional ideas about the most basic work behaviors of good journalists and good teachers are changing before our eyes.

The AP, which hired its first "automation editor" in 2015, has said it plans to use automated writing to cover more than 10,000 minor league baseball games annually.[2] It has already committed to producing most of its US corporate earnings stories this way.[3] And it is not the only news organization looking to automation: Forbes now relies on software from Narrative Science, a Chicago-based competitor to Automated Insights, to produce earnings reports. *The Los Angeles Times* now routinely alerts readers about earthquakes using a bot that composes tweets and brief stories based on US Geological Survey alerts. *The Washington Post* has developed its own "intelligent, automated storytelling agent," called Heliograf, which every four years automatically publishes the results of every Olympic event and, more consequentially, every single race in the US on election night.[4] Shailesh Prakash, vice president of digital product development at *The Post*, envisions Heliograf moving beyond pro forma stuff to actual story selection, searching the web to find out what people are talking about—Automated Insights is working on a similar tool—then checking to see if someone at the *Post* is covering it. If not, it could alert editors or just write the story itself—in seconds.[5]

A decade ago, Kristian Hammond, a Narrative Science cofounder, said that by 2026, "more than 90 percent" of news articles will be written algorithmically.[6] He also said we'd see a computer win a Pulitzer Prize by 2016, which is patently ridiculous until you realize that this is almost exactly what happened in 2016, when a worldwide consortium of 400 journalists at more than a hundred news organizations won said Pulitzer with reporting that analyzed 2.6 terabytes of data, supported by a powerful search algorithm that analyzed and cross-referenced 11.5 million documents.[7] That year, *Bloomberg* editor-in-chief John Micklethwait told the news organization's staff that automation "is crucial to the future of journalism in a much broader way than many of us realize. Done properly, automated journalism has the potential to make all our jobs more interesting."[8]

Automated platforms are also quietly turning the idea of mass publishing on its head. Narrative Science has long offered parents of Little League players the opportunity to enter game statistics into a smartphone app called GameChanger and receive a personalized account of their kids' games.[9] Wordsmith, Automated Insights' software platform, actually developed its reputation—and initially got AP's attention—by generating personalized, one-of-a-kind fantasy football recaps for millions of Yahoo! users.[10] It has since begun working with video game maker Activision to produce personalized recaps of players' *Call of Duty* matches, a strategy that Adam Smith, Automated Insights' chief operating officer, calls "mass personalization."[11]

The strategy makes a kind of perverse, inverted sense. If the goal is to attract a million readers, there are two basic ways to do it: the traditional way (produce one story that gets a million page views) or the reverse (produce a million stories with just one page view apiece). Smith in late 2018 said the million-stories strategy was actually just a starting point. "We're telling a story for every single one of their fantasy football players every single week, so millions of stories a week," he said.[12]

Before its switch to automation, the AP was producing 300 to 400 brief, formulaic earnings reports per quarter, said Jim Kennedy, senior vice president of strategy and enterprise development: "It's a drag, not just on the business news staff but on the entire operation of the AP. In order to cover as many companies as we were trying to cover, you had to leverage pretty much everybody who could pick up some slack around earnings time."

The traditional way of doing things had little to show. "We needed all hands on deck four times a year to cover earnings," he said. "And we were only able, with all of that effort—leveraging the entire AP—we were only able to cover 300 or 400 companies every earnings season, which is really only a small percentage of the entire stock market. We weren't getting anywhere close to covering the entire stock market. So, we were ceding that ground to everybody else. We were dragging down the entire operation four times a year, for several weeks."

Kennedy had seen technology that turned "structured data" into narrative text, but he was not impressed. Then, in 2013, colleagues in the news department showed him the Automated Insights fantasy football recaps, as well as a newsletter it was producing for the Cleveland Indians. He admitted, more than five years later, that the system passed a kind of on-the-fly Turing test. "I could not tell that the content was written by a machine," he said. "It blew me away."[13]

Kennedy decided to put the software through an "acid test" to see what it could handle: each week the AP would upload NFL data to produce brief 150- to 200-word stories on every one of the league's offensive players, all 300, paired with a constantly updated statistical ranking. "It was a job that no one would ever want to do," Kennedy said. "And it would be almost impossible for humans to do in a timely way."

The narratives and ranking were "flawless," Kennedy said, prompting him to push for the AP to automate earnings reports. "We knew, based on the NFL test, that we could do something of industrial strength, size, and scope." Once they did, the AP's earnings output grew tenfold overnight, with reduced error rates. After that came minor league baseball. "We're emancipating the journalists from work that no one really wants to do—and really don't expect to do when they come to work at a place like the AP," Kennedy said. "They expect they're going to cover big stories and they end up doing this menial labor."[14]

Wordsmith is now routinely expected to produce in excess of a billion stories a year, more than every other media outlet in the world combined. Those include, improbably, personalized reports that will never appear in any newspaper, including many that use GPS data from tracking devices worn by elderly customers. Automated Insights has partnered with a device maker to send users' family members brief narratives that alert them if their elderly relative is sticking to an established routine—visiting the grocery store or library, playing bridge with friends on Wednesdays, and the like. If a loved one stops doing these things, the algorithm alerts the audience— sometimes just one or two doting adult children in far-flung cities—that the narrative has changed.[15]

Perhaps most significantly, journalism in the near future will almost certainly face a growing credibility crisis due to the rise of actual fake news. In 2019, an effort backed by a handful of Silicon Valley titans began producing prose so convincing that critics began calling it "deepfakes for text." The tool, called GPT-2, needed just a few words to begin writing sentences based on its predictions of what should come next. It was quickly recognized as so dangerous that its creators, the nonprofit OpenAI, balked at releasing the full set of research to the public until they could figure out "the ramifications of the technological breakthrough."[16]

In one demonstration, programmers fed GPT-2 the first few paragraphs of a *Guardian* story about Brexit and it produced a passable fake newspaper story, complete with fabricated quotes from Labour Party Leader Jeremy Corbyn, as well as references to borders in Ireland and a made-up, entirely believable statement from Prime Minister Theresa May's spokesman: "Asked to clarify the reports, a spokesman for May said: 'The PM has made it absolutely clear her intention is to leave the EU as quickly as is possible and that will be under her negotiating mandate as confirmed in the Queen's speech last week.'"[17] All of it was completely made up.

In separate demonstrations, the tool also generated a fake news piece on the discovery by scientists of unicorns in the Andes and another on the theft of nuclear materials near Cincinnati.[18] Based on just a single sentence, GPT-2 wrote seven believable paragraphs that end with a nearly pitch-perfect quote from Tom Hicks, the fake US Energy Secretary: "The safety of people, the environment, and the nation's nuclear stockpile is our highest priority," Hicks said. "We will get to the bottom of this and make no excuses."[19]

For good measure, it also created a dutiful six-paragraph news brief about Miley Cyrus being caught shoplifting at an Abercrombie & Fitch on Hollywood Boulevard and, because this is America, it transcribed the election-night victory speech of a resurrected sci-fi John F. Kennedy—the prompt asked the computer to deliver remarks from a version of JFK who won reelection after his brain was "rebuilt from his remains and installed in the control center of a state-of-the-art humanoid robot." The reanimated JFK, it must be said, was as eloquent as ever: "In the months and years to come, there will be many battles in which we will have to be strong, and we must give all of our energy, not to repel invaders, but rather to resist aggression and to win the freedom and the equality for all of our people. The destiny of the human race hangs in the balance; we cannot afford for it to slip away."[20]

What these developments mean is, at this point, anyone's guess. But they all point to a new way of understanding the role of automation in journalism, one that belies the "robots will take our jobs" narrative to a more complicated, fraught, and, in some ways, more promising one: Robots will take your most loathsome tasks and create new kinds of content in the process—if we can keep them from producing an endless stream of cheaply manufactured trash.

As with nearly every other kind of automation, these developments challenge us to consider how human traits make an endeavor work. Once the most basic, loathsome transcription-heavy tasks are outsourced, human journalists must face the question: *What do I bring to this partnership?* A human reporter will always beat AI at talking to skittish sources, it seems, at cajoling details from a reluctant desk sergeant, or at figuring out the bigger picture. A human, unlike an algorithm, can also take a grieving widow by the hand, sit in her kitchen over a cup of hot tea, and listen to her story. And, of course, she can detect bullshit when she sees it.

Tools like Wordsmith and GPT-2 also challenge us to become better versions of ourselves, to expand our abilities and skills and think past the basic functions of journalism. In a way, this moment resembles the one fifty years ago when banks began installing ATMs. Though we tend to forget, the acronym "ATM" means "Automated Teller Machine." But banks didn't fire tellers en masse in the 1960s and 1970s. Boston University economist James Bessen has pointed out that since ATMs allowed them to operate branch offices more cheaply, with fewer human tellers per location, banks opened *more* branches, and the total number of tellers grew. But these new employees couldn't get by just by counting money—that skill was now outsourced in all but a few situations. They needed marketing skills, since they were now called upon not just to handle cash but to sell financial products, such as mortgages, car loans, and investment accounts.[21] And consider where the ATM aftermath went horribly wrong: a major bank began creating fake accounts for its customers in a shameful episode that *Bloomberg* opinion columnist Matt Levine—presumably a real person—in 2018 called "one of the highest-profile cases of banking villainy since the financial crisis."[22]

Journalists, who have always clung proudly to a scrappy, blue-collar sensibility, must now consider what sets them apart from their descendants. It's no longer good enough to be a good reporter—you've got to be a data journalist or a watchdog journalist, a visual journalist, able to explain a complicated concept to a curious audience. You've got to program, produce graphics and podcasts, and manipulate datasets. The German journalist Johannes Klingebiel has urged journalists not to think of the kind of automatic text generation that Wordsmith produces as "robot journalism"—while this will certainly have its place in the future, he predicts that imitation won't be the single defining use of AI in the newsroom. As with the Panama Papers effort, which Klingebiel's newsroom led, we'll likely see more cases in which AI helps journalists who are willing to work alongside it—he dubs these brave souls "centaur-journalists," from the Kasparov-inspired centaur chess developed in the late 1990s that was "faster, more precise, and more accessible to amateurs, than normal chess." What will always be left to humans to figure out, he has written, is what the data means, how it fits into "a messy and complex multi-polar world which has to be carefully explored and questioned."[23]

IN THE CLASSROOM

For classroom teachers, the corollary to Greg's benumbing box scores is exam preparation and grading. Few teachers relish the time they need to spend designing tomorrow's pop quiz, next week's cumulative unit test, or the end-of-term test. It is the rare pedagogue, indeed, who, at the sunset of her career, cherishes the memories of long weekends at the kitchen table spent grading student papers. Much of it is rote, repetitive, and dull, as students' answers rarely tend to be infused with surprising insight or flourishes of brilliance; generally, one paper after another hews closely and cautiously to what has been covered in the classroom—in other words, to what the students think the teacher wants to hear. And that may well be what the teacher wants to hear they have learned, but it doesn't allay the monotony of reading through hours of regurgitative content.

It is fair to say that there is a working consensus among educators that preparing and grading tests is the most unedifying time sink in a typical academic year. What's more, there is the hope that, if otherwise freed from the shackles of those grading hours, most committed teachers could and would use that time more richly designing deep team and personalized learning experiences for students.

The challenge has long been that grading—and certainly exam preparation—generally require just enough intellectual understanding to render those tasks intractable to previously available technology. Perhaps the best relief recent tech has been able to proffer is the means to scan multiple-choice bubble answers for automated scoring, but most *thick* learning cannot be assessed in such a facile fashion as multiple-choice exams, especially in the humanities.

It is perhaps no surprise, then, that a substantial portion of the AI applications to classroom practice currently focuses on exam preparation and assessment of student essays. These technologies are benefitting from neural net processing and from machine learning algorithms. They can work toward a satisfactory outcome from several vectors. Some are built around reading through many thousands of essays in order to identify the key words and even ideas that mark a successful essay. This is much the same process as is used in teaching a program to craft its own automated written answer to the question—or to write a game recap built around box scores—only, in this case, it is used not to write a robo-answer but, rather, to robo-assess student answers.

Another approach is to provide the algorithm with model essays, helping it to identify what makes them successful, and then programming it to apply this model as scaffolding by which to judge the efficacy of actual student essays—somewhat akin to a Chomskyan approach to language acquisition. Other approaches, too, are in development, and some programs combine approaches to optimize the application, but the point is that the robots are becoming every day more adroit at grading written exams, a skill long considered the unquestioned redoubt of human intelligence.

While, to date, the results are decidedly mixed, the general consensus is that the robots are not yet quite as good as human teachers at grading, but that they are getting remarkably close to parity with humans. Many current users prefer, if scale allows, to take a blended approach—allowing the robot to do the first runthrough and then refining those results via perusal of the essays by the teacher. Everyone, however, agrees, that the programs are improving rapidly, and most see the day of robo-grading, sans humans or perhaps with only cursory human teacher oversight, as rapidly approaching. Worth noting: One area in which the robots are already far beyond human educators is their capacity to simultaneously scan millions of databases while grading essays to check for plagiarism.

It is easy to see both the need for—and ready application of—such AI grading systems for online education programs that often operate on vast scales. (The enrollment in massive open online courses, also known as MOOCs, now regularly runs into the tens of thousands.) Yet they are soon going to be ubiquitous in classrooms large and small across the land.

Today's narrow AI is also already being applied to help teachers generate exam questions. The process for generating questions would be familiar to those working in the field of AI-generated journalism, such as Greg's liberating box score bot—deep learning from large datasets coupled with modeling of ideal types. Teachers, at this stage at least, no doubt check the questions generated before passing them along to students for exams, but, so far, the results are promising for at least generic unit summation types of questions.

And improvements are likely to develop rapidly, as a welter of research is being applied in this direction, enriched and informed by similar applications in other fields, such as journalism. The nineteenth international conference on Artificial Intelligence in Education, convened in London in the summer of 2018, for instance, included presentations with such titles as "Measuring the Quality of Assessment Using Questions Generated from the Semantic Web," "How Should Knowledge Composed of Schemas Be Represented in Order to Optimize Student Model Accuracy?," "Active Learning for Improving Machine Learning of Student Explanatory Essays," and even "Towards Combined Network and Text Analytics of Student Discourse in Online Discussions"—all areas that promise to liberate classroom practitioners from some, if not most, of the more laborious aspects of writing and grading tests.[24]

Far from replacing teachers or eliminating classroom jobs, the hope and promise of these applications, of course, is that teachers will be freed up from their more arduous, time-consuming, and unedifying tasks so that they can concentrate their time on interventions that most effectively utilize their considerable talents as educators and optimize student learning outcomes. One can readily imagine dedicated master teachers using their preparation time on deeper professional development, networking with innovative colleagues online, and creating lessons that enhance student engagement. Obversely, the downside risk, of course, is that districts will view the time freed up from test preparation and grading as an opportunity to increase teacher loads, resulting in no or even negative learning improvement. One can hardly be faulted for feeling less than sanguine about the pressures on district leaders.

On a higher pedagogical plane, current AI research promises education applications that can help teachers actually be more effective as teachers in the classroom. Integration of sophisticated visual sensing with real-time machine assessment and feedback is leading to systems that will inform a teacher continuously throughout the day how she or he is moving about the classroom or monitor the quality of students' teamwork dynamics.[25]

Jim has also seen multiple tools in various research labs that use relatively unobtrusive devices to monitor students' neural oscillations (i.e., "brain waves") to display their attentiveness at any given moment in a lesson; these devices are coupled with tools that allow teachers to aggregate the entire class or individuate, isolate, identify separate students' attention. At its best, such a tool might well help educators continually assess and improve upon lessons in which student engagement appears to lapse. There is, however, a host of critical questions educators must ask of this technology—including the perhaps not immediately obvious question of whether attentiveness equates to learning. For instance, what if a student, in a moment of reflectiveness, synthesizes important concepts, only to have the device scan this state as inattentiveness? At its worst, it is not difficult to imagine a dystopian image of children virtually chained to a machine monitoring their cognitive performances like so many bots.

There is, nonetheless, also great potential for a blended AI/teacher classroom marked by a high degree of personalization in student learning. One interesting area of AI applications to education is in what is termed "cold start" predictive AI. This involves developing algorithms that can quickly scale up an assessment of an individual student's learning strengths, weaknesses, and style as soon as possible from knowing nothing about that particular student (i.e., "cold start"), with as few early data points as possible. It is rather akin to the famous Guinness t-test in statistics (Yes, beer once again moved civilization forward![26]), but on steroids and in real time. Not surprisingly, it is seen as particularly applicable to MOOCs, as those online venues can include tens of thousands of students about whom the teacher knows nothing; cold start predictive AI holds the promise to be able to personalize the MOOC experience for all of those students after little of the class has actually transpired, based upon early limited assessment analysis.

Interestingly, though, this might prove entirely unnecessary when encryption technologies improve to the point of making practicable a central repository of every person's entire lifelong learning portfolio. Blockchain may already facilitate such a development, though quantum encryption will likely provide the watershed breakthrough. Imagine that every person could maintain a thoroughly secure cloud-based repository of his or her education assessments and achievements, including emblematic samples of completed work, which has been aggregating since childhood. When signing up for, say, a MOOC to polish or develop new skills at midcareer, the course processor could receive permission to access this database for an immediate, thoroughgoing AI-informed assessment of how to optimize that individual's learning experience and outcomes via highly personalized delivery of class materials and activities, based upon a lifetime's accumulated "hot start." No need in this scenario for cold starts.

The key takeaway from this brief foray into the congeries of ways in which AI technologies are beginning to encroach on the realm of both traditional and emergent education practices is similar to Greg's lesson in journalism. If we as educators and as a society curate these tools responsibly, they could dramatically free teachers from the baser "administrivia" that weigh like an albatross around their time in the current state of the profession, freeing them up to do what they can best provide: charismatic, caring, and nurturing teaching of students. Further coupling these comparatively liberated teachers with blended AI tools for personalizing learning with increasing sophistication will assuredly lead to greater teacher satisfaction and improved student engagement, with concomitant positive and demonstrable learning outcomes. As the tech writer Kevin Kelly has said, "Let the robots take our jobs, and let them help us dream up new work that matters."[27]

The downside risk—to be resisted—is that society will force shortcuts as AI makes possible ever greater loads on teachers spread increasingly thin across larger numbers of students receiving minimal attention from actual humans.

THE THREE Cs: CREATING

As Bellamy and Rumple walk between classrooms, Rumple confides to her, "I have to say, though the technology I'm seeing is remarkable, I actually haven't heard or seen anything yet that, pedagogically speaking, strikes me as truly revolutionary. Those creatures in terraria were dazzling, but I recall that, in my day, we were dabbling with genetic engineering, too. Teachers could even download lesson plans on how to help young children extract DNA from a strawberry."

"Good point," says Bellamy. "Even with all these thorough-going changes in recent years, there really is nothing entirely new under the sun. After all, there have been student-centered learning models discussed since at least Rousseau's *Emile* and certainly by such founders and innovators as Maria Montessori or John Dewey. The point is not that what we do now is unprecedented or unfamiliar. Rather, it's a shift in emphasis. What was once the focus of most school hours, such as content acquisition, has been somewhat attenuated and decentralized while other skills, equally familiar but historically marginal to the core curriculum, have taken center stage. The very antiquity of these skills made them easier to integrate at the center of our new learning, both because they were not revolutionary and because there were already excellent models for implementation that had been developed over decades. Our project-based learning approach, for instance, is far from unprecedented, so teachers were able to adjust and embrace the change in emphases confidently and smoothly. In fact, when we first brought these curricular developments to schools, it was actually the primary school teachers who felt most comfortable. They were the early adopters who quickly became mentors to many of the secondary-level faculty."

"Fascinating," Rumple says. "Because the new models were so similar to long-established lower-school teaching methods?"

"Precisely. In those early days, we jokingly referred to our initiative as the 'kindergartenization' of the entire school, across every grade.[28] But there are skills we now strive to provide every student that might not be quite so recognizable to you. 'Capacity to retain depth and linearity of rational analysis amid electronic distractibility,' for instance."

"That makes sense," Rumple agrees.

"Or 'comfort with accelerating change,'" Bellamy continues. "Or 'cybercurating ethics,'" she adds.

"Cyber—what?"

"Cybercurating ethics," says Bellamy. "This may take some explaining. It's really part of the overall Three Cs economy." Holding up her hand to forestall Rumple's obvious next question, Bellamy proceeds: "Let me explain: In the 2020s, researchers achieved a general consensus that the digital revolution, especially in the areas of robotics and AI, was going to bring about a vast shift on the same scale as the Industrial Revolution, but that it was going to transpire over less than half a century—perhaps only twenty-five years."

"I remember there was a lot of discussion about that just before I dozed off," says Rumple, "but the consensus you describe hadn't arrived yet. People were still arguing over the question of whether this period would be the same or different from previous epochs of technological change."

"Precisely. I remember that as well," says Bellamy. "It became clear just a short time into the third decade that many jobs would be eliminated by smart machines—jobs like truck drivers and pharmacists, even financial analysts—that were readily and rapidly automated. People panicked a bit about whether there would be any jobs left. This led to calls for legislation to outlaw the adoption or slow down the research and development of AI or bots. But cooler heads prevailed, pointing out that slowing down technology adoption would be the surest bet to eliminate jobs permanently, since other countries like China were certainly not going to stop modernizing their economies.

"Eventually, public policy shifted to embrace a close partnership between industry and government to implement a more intentional grand plan to educate and shift people into jobs that were a complement to machines—or toward jobs that machines couldn't do, or that we simply didn't want them to do."

"Really?" Rumple asks. "People sure weren't looking to government for leadership up until I can remember."

"True," says Bellamy, "but Americans tend to rise to the occasion when times demand it, and people realized that such a massive change, taking place over so short a time, couldn't just be left to sort itself out if we wanted to avoid massive social, political, and economic convulsions. The digital revolution was about to impact, disrupt, or eliminate so many jobs at once that we needed real leadership to create new jobs and to train people for them ASAP. That was when government and corporate leaders got together—and they invited experts from education, healthcare, and many other fields to a series of summits in Washington. Out of those came the initiative we now call the 'Three Cs' economy: creating, cybercurating, and caring. Most of the jobs we've created to ensure full employment over the past couple decades fall somewhere in those categories. And they're the jobs that people can do better than even the smartest machines or that are best done by people and bots working as partners."

"I'm not sure I understand quite what you mean when you say that some jobs are best done with machines and people as partners," says Rumple.

"You were already doing it for most of your life," she says. "As I said when we visited that first classroom, every time you used a computer or a smart phone to do your job better, you were a collective intelligence with the machine, or what I prefer to call a collaborative intelligence. You and the computer or phone were augmenting each other, both doing what you did best to create an optimal pairing so the best job performance could happen. You did it naturally and adjusted accordingly as each generation of computers got better. You were even a collaborative intelligence when you were using a hand calculator in school."

"But those machines weren't able to think or understand anything!" Rumple protests.

"Hmmm," Bellamy muses, somewhat cryptically. "That's a hard one, and we're still debating that question. Certainly, it seems safe to say that a hand calculator wasn't sentient, but even that primitive device did some things that humans had always associated with intelligence—and it did them far faster and more accurately than any person ever could. As artificial intelligence has gotten, well, more intelligent over the years, it's become harder and harder to say that the bots don't think. Certainly, even today, if they do think, they don't think like us, but neither does my dog—yet I'm sure she thinks in her doggy way. On some level, it doesn't matter. The real point is that bots today do innumerable intelligent tasks better, faster, and more consistently than we do. Our best hope is to work in collaboration with them. And we've found that doing so ensures more and better productivity than either working alone."

"Interesting that you mention productivity," Rumple inquires, "because there was talk by some pundits of a new era about to dawn of human leisure and of everyone being given a universal income when AI matured."

"Right—that was actually tried in some countries, but it mostly failed," Bellamy says. "Particularly in Scandinavia. About ten years ago, after a long lag, productivity from smart automation finally really took off. With lots of jobs being taken over by bots and with productivity so high, some leaders argued that people no longer needed to work for a living and that it made sense to give everyone a guaranteed income so that they could support themselves—and also so that there would continue to be enough consumers with money in their pockets to keep the postemployment economy healthy."

"Sounds pretty good to me," says Rumple. "Why on earth did it fail?"

"We found that most people need—and even want—work to feel fulfilled and to feel that their lives have meaning. The populations with UGI tended pretty quickly to be saddled with heavy drug and alcohol abuse. Violence, too. The general feeling, at least here in the US, was that people needed work, even if their material needs could be provided by machines. So, we rallied around creating the Three Cs economy to give every able person a job. We also found that work shared by bots and people as collaborators was completed much more successfully and creatively, leading to markedly greater economic growth than in societies that settled for UGI at lower productivity and standards."

"So, the Three Cs stand for caring, cyber-, um, what, again?"

"Creating, cybercurating, and caring," Bellamy laughs.

"Right," Rumple nods, grinning sheepishly and a bit red-faced. "Can you take me through those a bit?"

"Of course. The creating job sector is probably the most familiar to you, but there is a fairly wide range of professions in there. In the creating sector, for instance, you'll find the entrepreneurs, the designers of new products, the visionaries. They tend to be highly educated and successful."

"And highly remunerated," Rumple adds knowingly.

"Well, yes, that's true," Bellamy concurs, "but they don't make more than others by as many multiples as they did in the earlier part of the century. Though it's certainly true that many of these jobs tend to be elite, there are other jobs in the creating sector that don't make as much but can be highly rewarding. Obviously, artists, writers, and musicians fall into this category."

"Of course," Rumple agrees.

"Self-performed poetry and storytelling at open mic nights have become all the rage. And, similar to what you saw in the library, a big art form these days is bioengineering new, exotic plants for display in biomuseums. Living art, created to suit the artistic vision or whimsy of the artist. Some of them are quite outlandish! There are also many more craftspeople today than when you dozed off twenty years ago. As machines have become more capable of making everything, and as productivity has put more money in everyone's pockets, there has been a big demand for human-made products. Everything from furniture to clothing to soap. It's more expensive, but somehow comforting to many people to know that they're buying something that has been created by another person."

Rumple chuckles. "You're describing almost exactly what happened with William Morris and the Arts and Crafts movement in the 1860s."

"Precisely," Bellamy says. "But it has really taken off lately."

As she speaks, Bellamy reaches behind her neck and pulls a long canvas tag from inside her sweater so Rumple can read it: *Handcrafted by humans.*

"Fascinating," he says.

6 WHAT IF SCHOOL WERE REAL LIFE?

The setting would intimidate anyone, let alone an eighteen-year-old: a twenty-ninth-story conference room in the downtown Philadelphia headquarters of Braskem America, the US arm of the Brazilian petrochemical giant. Yet, one-by-one, students stride into the room, stand before a group of executives, and politely—if nervously—ask for money to heal the world.

It's a bitterly cold afternoon in mid-February, and the seventeen students, seniors at Science Leadership Academy, a nearby magnet high school, are all deep into research on their capstones, yearlong projects designed to solve a sticky problem each has identified. The students hail from all over Philadelphia—the school prides itself on embracing every zip code in the city. Earlier this afternoon, they walked the half-mile from school, joking and chattering the whole way. Now, escorted upstairs under heavy security, they've shed their coats and stand self-possessed and well dressed as they introduce themselves to a shark-tank gathering of Braskem officials. Each young person quickly clicks through a set of PowerPoint slides, making the case for small grants to move their projects along.

The scene, complete with a commanding view of City Hall as the sun sets over the century-old statue of William Penn,

could be right out of a movie. But as judges listen to each con-
testant, they begin to identify a pattern, a small, if obvious,
problem: the students aren't asking for enough money.

One wants $400 to build portable roll-up beds of nylon
rope and strips of recycled tires for the homeless. Another
wants exactly $403.75 to edit and publish an anthology of
stories that will encourage teens going through hard times. "I
don't like counseling," she says. "I've never liked counseling."
She has already lined up eighteen coauthors and plans to give
away copies of the book.

Another asks for $290 "plus tax" for materials to conduct
free art workshops for seniors suffering from dementia. Yet
another wants just $240 to write, shoot, and edit a documen-
tary about teens and mental health—it'll be free to watch on
YouTube.

In nearly every case, the judges listen, consider each student's ask, then politely but firmly suggest: Maybe you could
ask us for more? Another couple hundred to promote this or
buy supplies?

Another classmate proclaims that she wants to extract oil
from algae, the green gunk in fish tanks, and refine it into biodiesel. She's asking for enough money to buy a fancy-looking,
closed-loop oil extractor. Price: $350.99. "And the shipping is
free," she says cheerfully. "So, who doesn't love that?" Also, she
says, it's designed to attach to a standard vacuum cleaner. Asked
where she'll get one, she blinks, incredulous: "My house?"

Finally, Chris Lehmann, the school's principal, rises to
address the judges. He has led this school since the beginning,
in 2006, and has seen hundreds of capstones—perhaps a thousand or more—go from idea to execution to full-blown reality. He applauds the students and reminds them of how much
they've matured since freshman year. Then he turns to thank
the judges and says, by way of explanation: "We have always
made something out of nothing."

In the age of automation, perhaps our best model for success will come from a place like this, a scrappy little magnet school whose students fully expect that they can change the world on a shoestring.

Science Leadership Academy, or SLA, as it's called, takes the idea of project-based learning as seriously as any high school in America. Then it takes that idea to its logical conclusion, asking: *Now what?*

SLA forces us to reconsider how we think about innovation and the future of high school. It forces us to rethink, down to the molecular level, how we approach motivation and the challenges that young people face. Perhaps most importantly, it sets itself apart by leapfrogging over the goals the typical American high school holds for most of its students. Forget finding a good, solid, nonautomatable, robot-proof job, Lehmann and his colleagues would say. That's a laudable goal, but it's simply not enough. You have to be a good citizen.

After all, "worker" is merely a subset of "citizen." If we aim for good citizens, he says, we'll get the workforce we need. If we only aim for good workers, we'll never get the citizens we need. In other words, he and those around him say, the best way to prepare students for a life alongside algorithms and automation is to make them knowledgeable, effective citizens who understand databases but who also know how to petition City Hall, read their grandmother's mortgage statement, interpret a nonprofit's 990, and identify a demagogue.[1]

Beyond the obvious clash of philosophies, there's a bit to unpack here. For one thing, the adults at SLA will tell you, an education built on what is today generally considered workforce development gives you rule-followers, not leaders, young people well versed in compliance, in adherence to rules. It delivers young people adept at living within strict hierarchies—a group, in other words, that's good at doing what they're told but not very good at discerning what to do with themselves. Focusing on citizenship yields young people who will question the rules and their underlying assumptions, who will be forever suspicious of hierarchies, not ready to join them.

That philosophical shift also cracks open a host of possibilities for a rich curriculum, turning the idea of "lifelong learning" on its head. "It's a lovely phrase," Lehmann says, but it doesn't go far enough—and it rings hollow if school is all about getting a job. Most jobs, after all, leverage just a narrow set of skills and knowledge. But citizenship requires more and leaves the door open to more possibilities.

"Lifelong learning," he might say, has by now acquired a patina of training and retraining, of retooling in service to the next set of someone else's work requirements. Even if that were school's job—and it's not, he might argue—it's a terrible motivator if we want students to work hard and take school seriously. "I think we have an obligation to always ask, 'Why does it matter?' and have a real answer to those questions. 'This is good for you someday' is *not* motivating."[2]

Perhaps, Lehmann says, we should start using the phrase "lifelong intellectuals," and get about the work of producing students who take more joy in the life of the mind. "I want kids to graduate here with their heads full of thought." Lehmann's "North Star" is the phrase "thoughtful, wise, passionate, and kind," he says. "I want them to have the wisdom to apply the thoughts in powerful ways. I want them to have the passion to push through when the world tells them they can't get it done, and I want them to be kind because, Jesus Christ, the world needs more of that."[3]

SLA subscribes informally to a philosophy known as "deeper learning," most notably detailed in a 2014 book of the same name, which says schools should prepare students to master essential academic content, think critically, work collaboratively, and solve complex problems. Most importantly, students should be the self-directed "leaders of their own educational lives."[4]

SLA takes the model a bit further than most "deep learning" schools, calling itself "inquiry-based." Perhaps most significantly, it obliterates education's long-understood concept of time, of then vs. now, of the very idea that high school is a "moratorium" for young people busy waiting out adolescence, as if it's some sort of holding pen designed to give them basic skills and keep them busy until they're old enough and mature enough to be functioning adults. Lehmann has by now become famous for challenging the received wisdom of high school as preparation for life, instead asking anyone who will listen: "*What if school were real life?*" Taking that seriously forces us to ask even more pointed questions, such as: *How would an eighteen-year-old function as a fully participating citizen?* And: *What should she do all day in school?*

The basic answer is that school should do everything it can to allow a student to play a kind of "junior varsity" version of life, one that looks very much like the one she'll soon inhabit, but with extra help, lower stakes, and an open-door policy to the adults who run the school.[5]

Anna Walker-Roberts, a digital video and photography teacher who moved to Philadelphia to teach at SLA after reading about it in *Deeper Learning*, says teachers regularly ask students for feedback about their lessons. Students, she says, soon begin to understand how the learning at SLA is designed. "And if it's done poorly, they'll complain about it." A recent professional development session, she says, was built on the results of a single student satisfaction survey.[6]

As a result, SLA's students are somehow both more focused on academics and more relaxed about them than most high schoolers, more open and engaged in the enterprise, and more willing than most to stop, think, and talk about what they're doing. Diana Laufenberg, one of SLA's earliest teachers, said a blend of "humanity and scholarly inquiry" fuels the proceedings.[7]

All the same, it's consuming, exhausting work. "We get smacked in the face by the stuff that we're trying to do that isn't working," Lehmann says. "And we kind of always remind ourselves that if this was easy, everybody would be doing it."[8]

The projects developed at SLA not only ask students to solve problems, as educator Jaime Casap says, but to make the solutions public. Implicit in a project is an audience—typically teachers, parents, and classmates, and perhaps even more people in a broader circle. By contrast, think about the audience for a test or written essay: It's one person, typically a teacher, evaluating the work at a separate address and in an undefined time frame. The grade is a strictly private matter—unless the score is high, in which case everybody can know. But if you are giving kids the opportunity to have a juried critique in public, anything is possible, from triumph to tragedy. And if they don't have the demonstration ready when the jury arrives, that's a big deal. As senior Gregory Tasik recently put it, "You don't want to look lackluster next to your classmates. You want to present something good."[9]

The theory behind projects is anything but mush-headed—rather, it's based on brain science, which says we remember things better by making associations. By asking students to do something authentic, teachers are creating several different pathways to learn the same material. Early SLA teacher Zac Chase says a project "asks the brain to kind of map ideas in a way that is much more connected and intricate and complex, so that the information is stored in multiple ways." It also gives students the opportunity to relate new experiences to ones they've already had.

And it's a more pleasurable experience than reading about something in a textbook or hearing it in a lecture. "Remembering facts tends to not make people want to go back and remember more facts," Chase says. "Think of the last time you learned something. It tends not to be a listing of facts or 'Oh, I built this background knowledge.' It was, 'Oh, I needed to figure out how to do this thing.' And so approaching challenges where kids need to figure out how to do things makes more sense."[10]

Perhaps the most important part of a project at SLA is that everyone isn't doing the same thing.

Walker-Roberts, the digital video teacher, says SLA fights against the common misperception that project-based learning is simply the act of having students make or build or do something, anything, without much thought. That's not what the school is chasing, a "Lego kits" undertaking in which every kid builds his or her version of the same model. "That's not inquiry-based," she says.[11]

As at Iowa BIG, another school we'll read about in a later chapter, Lehmann and Chase suggest inviting local organizations into classrooms to outline the problems they face, then help students build solutions. "There's no need for the teachers to manufacture problems," they write. "The world will take care of that."[12]

For his part, Chase says he never asks teenagers what their "passions" are. The question seems logical for an inquiry-based, project-based school, but he says it's unfair. "Asking anybody, let alone somebody with a newly forming prefrontal cortex, 'What are you passionate about?' is an overwhelming and daunting task," he says. "What am *I* passionate about? What are *you* passionate about?"

There's a finality to that inquiry that's intimidating, Chase says. Rather, he asks students: *What are you curious about?* "It's a much more accessible question. 'Passion' just feels like it comes with some stakes that are unfair. The learning should be daunting—not the choosing."[13]

Chase left SLA in spring 2011 for a master's degree at the Harvard Graduate School of Education. He later spent three years at the US Department of Education at the end of the Obama administration. He's now a language arts coordinator for a school district in Colorado—he jokes that, working at SLA, he fretted about 150 kids whose problems kept him up at night. Now he frets about 32,000. "You want to talk about solving puzzles . . ."[14]

Tweaks like the ones that he and Lehmann and others have made help make SLA one of the few high schools in America where an adult can spend time and want to return, not flee. Visit John Kamal's engineering class and you'll see students building, soldering, troubleshooting, and operating the classroom's well-used 3-D printer and laser cutter.

"We use automated tools now instead of handcrafting," he says (although he admits to doing a bit of handcrafting with ninth graders). "Instead of teaching them drafting, I teach them about scaling. The essential thing that I want them to understand is about models, and scaling models, because that can be applied to a wide range of different topics and areas."[15]

Visit Matthew Kay's English class and you'll see students writing nearly all the time. "We're teaching them how to think," he says, sitting just outside the classroom while his students read from books they've chosen that morning. "And if you do that, then machinery is not going to replace you. If you're teaching thinking, that's the permanent stuff. But we can be replaced, and maybe even *should* be replaced, if all we're teaching is dates, names, facts, and stuff that they can Google. If the high end of what we're teaching is what happened on page 34, then we are obsolete."[16]

If students aren't writing a lot, he says, you're wasting everyone's time.

"I'll hear of some schools and some classes where the kids will write one essay in the year. What are you *doing*? What, literally, are you doing for all of the days that you're doing? How are you not writing five essays, six essays, *seven essays*? How are you not writing four stories, five stories, two poetry collections? *How are your kids not writing?* What on earth are you doing in that classroom all day?" When colleagues at other schools boast that their students work hard writing two big essays a year, Kay listens, thinking that by mid-February, "My ninth graders have written like four, five by now."[17]

Lehmann has written that educators should rethink the most basic qualities of their relationships with students, treating teacher and student behaviors not as two different things but as one thing "on a continuum." When educators begin to see students, and the ways they behave, as more similar to them and the way they behave, he writes, they can look at consequences "in a far more humanistic way."[18]

While there are obvious differences between the maturity—and the actions—of a fifteen-year-old and a forty-year-old, our motivations and responses (and our obvious faults) are similar, he writes, and more accurately plotted along this continuum. "And that should help us forgive more quickly, seek to punish less frequently, and be willing to understand more deeply."[19]

For instance, he asks the teacher with the strict late-work policy to consider whether the secretary "has to chase him down for his attendance every day."[20] Likewise, the principal who's annoyed by loud students in the lunchroom should stop to remember that he laughs just as raucously at faculty luncheons.[21] He suggests that teachers who cling to strict behavioral policies or draconian deadlines do so because they are, in a sense, like flight attendants on a commercial airliner who strenuously insist that passengers stow their tray tables and bring their seats to an upright position: it's not imperative for landing the plane, but it's one of the few things still within their control.

In fall 2019, the school took up new quarters a few miles away, but as in the old building, Lehmann's office still sits near the entrance, where it is harder to avoid him than to be seen by him. Then as now, the teachers' lounge sits immediately behind his office with a doorway connecting the two rooms. In the original building, the door jamb soon became worn paintless by teachers who would rest their shoulders there while stopping by to talk, and it will likely happen again.

Try to engage Lehmann in conversation and, for one thing, you'll never hear an unadulterated, complete sentence. You'll be interrupted often—his office door is almost never closed, and someone is always entering, leaving, or passing through. But once he gets started, Lehmann talks constantly about what he calls SLA's "ethic of care," an overarching philosophy that captures the many different ways in which adults look out for students. "Kids have the rest of their lives to learn the world is a cruel and horrible place," he says. "They shouldn't learn it from us."

Shana Bergmann, the SLA senior who wants to refine bio-fuel from algae, showed up as a freshman in the fall of 2015, just two years after moving to the city with her mother from the South Mountain area of Phoenix. Bergmann's parents had been divorced for years and she was happy in her tiny, progressive, Montessori-based charter elementary school, which featured yoga and gardening and grew its own food for snack time. But by the time she was in middle school, the district had begun cutting art and music programs and threatening a four-day school week. "I thought that was offensive," she says. "So, I spoke up about it to my mom, who was only really there because she didn't want to take me away from my father." Eventually they decided to move to Philly, where her mother had family roots. Shana was 13 and had never spent much time in a big city. Friends urged her to apply to SLA, and the next thing she knew, she was being called in for an interview.

Once accepted, she focused on engineering—the concentration demands three to four hours of engineering class per day, for all four years. "My eyes just opened up to a whole new world," she says. "I felt like everything was coming together. Finally, math was being applied and ethics was being applied, and there is a right and wrong to ethical questions, and there is a way to teach that."

She came upon the algae project while volunteering at a local environmental nonprofit and thinking about sustainability—especially what it looks like in low-income communities. Every year, she says, American industry consumes about sixty-three million gallons of diesel fuel. The extraction rate of an acre of algae is ten thousand gallons, which can be harvested after just ten days. If we grew just six million acres of algae, she says, "we could meet that goal in ten days—literally. So that's really interesting to me."[22]

Six million acres isn't exactly a tiny parcel of land—about the size of Vermont, actually. But compared to the size of a few western states, it's minuscule. Such an expanse would equal just over 3 percent of the total acreage of Texas, for example.

Economies as small as Puerto Rico's or as large as Brazil's could benefit from making biodiesel out of algae "because it's such a quick process, it's so reliable, it's predictable because it's scalable. And it's so environmentally friendly," Bergmann says. "You know, we're not drilling, we're not using resources that took millions of years to make. We're using resources that took ten days to make. That's a huge difference." Also, a byproduct of the refining process, she says, is glycerine soap, which she plans to package and give away (despite a Braskem executive's suggestion that she sell it to underwrite the biofuel extraction).

"The real sellable point for me is how scalable it is," she says. "You know, small communities anywhere can grow their own algae, extract the oil, and do a simple chemical process. I would like to standardize that process so it's a bit safer for them."[23]

She tells the shark tank judges, "If you're growing your own algae and you know how much you have, you can just scale it

up. This could be used in economies that are underdeveloped—
and a small community could be utilizing this. Or a huge plant
could be growing all this algae. And the scalability is really, I
think, the main selling point on my project. It could be helping small communities *and* the global market."

The Braskem judges listen to her pitch and a few days later
offer to buy her the fancy-looking extractor—they're also
willing to pair her with an energy consultant and throw in a
calorimetry setup so she can test the project's fuel economy.
Bergmann agrees and offers to donate the calorimetry rig to
the school once she graduates.

As for the vacuum cleaner, she eventually relents, allowing
Braskem to buy her one—she says it's probably a good idea. Her
mother's vacuum cleaner is probably not the best tool for the
job. "I have a sixteen-pound cat," she says. "It's full of cat hair."

Lehmann says projects like Shana's go directly to the heart
of what high school should look like, not just for students
like Shana but for everyone. "'Why do I need to know this?'
should be a real question. And the answers we should search
out for kids should not be 'someday' answers: 'If you want to
major in *this*, you might seek out this information,' but rather,
'Why do I need this information now to be a better human
being? To affect change in the world?'"[24]

THE THREE Cs: CYBERCURATING

"The cybercurating sector will probably be the least familiar to you, so that will take some explaining," Bellamy says. "This really has three subsets, only one of which you'll likely recognize: cyberethical inputs, cybersecurity, and cyberethical outcomes assessment. Cybersecurity is not much different today from what you would have known, though the role of people in that area is much less than before, because the defensive programs utilizing AI have gotten so sophisticated. Cyberethical inputs, on the other hand, is an almost entirely new field that came into its own with the widespread adoption of driverless cars in the 2020s. Those cars really are intelligent machines, and it was recognized early on that they were having to make ethical choices."

"Ethical?" Rumple asks, confused.

"Sure," Bellamy says. "The cars sometimes had to make the same split-second decisions as human drivers, such as whether to hit an adult in the crosswalk or a child chasing a ball into the street, if both can't be avoided in time. The more autonomous cars there were on the road, the more situations with ethical dilemmas presented themselves, which meant that jobs were created for people to preprogram the value parameters by which the AI programs in cars should make such decisions. That led pretty quickly to an entire industry of people, in academia, in government, in corporations, who were examining what ethical values should inform cyber decision making more generally, because AI was starting to be embedded in everything, the Internet of Things, even weaponry."

"Weaponry?"

"Lethal Autonomous Weapons Systems, or LAWS, really caught the public's attention and scared the heck out of everybody. The idea that machines would be making decisions about whom to kill in battle unnerved millions and led to a flood of funding for cyberethics positions."

"Why not just have humans make the decisions from a distance, as with drones?" asks Rumple.

"That makes sense, and that was precisely the approach taken in the developmental stages of LAWS. No weapon, no matter how intelligent, was allowed to take any lethal action without a human decision point, but that disappeared the first time American LAWS came up against similar weapons of another country that did not share those compunctions. The adversary's weapons, allowed to be truly autonomous, assessed changing battlefield situations and adjusted tactics in nanoseconds, completely obliterating our weapons, which were waiting for humans in Colorado to authorize a strike."

"Oh, I see," Rumple says.

"If we wanted to keep up or even have a chance against such an adversary, it was clear that our weapons needed to be let loose to make their own split-second decisions, too. That was the real impetus behind wholesale adoption of cyberethical inputs as a major field of study and employment. And that changed everything in education."

"In education? How, exactly?"

"Well, for one, it led to a reaffirmation of the humanities curriculum at the center of K–12 education. Before that, there had been a consuming focus on STEM in the curricular reforms of the early twenty-first century. A bit later, many reformers started to include the arts along with science, technology, engineering, and mathematics, which they called STEAM, but, really, this was still just a science and technology focus. The arts component of those curricula tended to be just an add-on or in the service of tech training, such as teaching product design or data infographics. But cyberethics education required a deep dive back into the humanities curriculum to find ways of approaching values in a complex, multicultural society. Some wag added the H for humanities to STEAM, scrambled the letters, and came up with what was called the THAMES Curriculum, which British educators loved, of course."

Rumple laughs. "Of course! The sign outside the school!"

"Yes," Bellamy says. "Sorry to confuse you. But THAMES also caught on here. That's still what we call it, though the students occasionally have a bit of fun with it. Last year, on April Fool's Day, one of the students used an online anagram generator and reprogrammed all of the signs to read, "Welcome to HA! STEM! Academy.""

"Brilliant."

"Indeed. But I should add that it's not exactly the humanities curriculum you would know."

"Oh?"

"Well, it is, and it isn't. In other words, it was focused and honed to meet very specific needs. Rather than just reading a classic work of literature or a poem, today's students are given readings that are carefully selected to raise key ethical issues and dilemmas. Our goal is not to provide bromides or easy solutions but to encourage students to think deeply from early ages about how to approach key challenges, especially how representative thinkers or groups would differently approach similar situations. Today's secondary students, for instance, are regularly asked to consider an ethical challenge and demonstrate genuine understanding of how it would be treated or resolved by Aristotle, utilitarians such as Bentham, various religious systems, Kantian imperatives, pragmatists, and so forth, so that they go into their life as cybercitizens and cyberworkers with a richly varied toolbox of approaches to new challenges."

"Does no one read just to be enriched as humans by great literature?" asks Rumple, furrowing his brow.

"Hopefully, all good teachers also impart that," Bellamy concurs, "but I can't say that's the chief focus of our THAMES curriculum mandates."

"You mentioned something about ethics and outcomes too, didn't you?" Rumple asks.

"Good memory! Cyberethical outcomes assessment (CEOA) really follows pretty straightforwardly from what we've been discussing—it just deals with humans applying values to assess the algorithms' output. Even when AI was very primitive and narrow, companies such as Facebook were noticing that some bias was creeping into their programs' outputs when they were crunching big data. Some biases stemmed from the unintentional bias programmers brought into their coding, while others emerged from the selection or availability of data, from biases in the society that were reflected in the data, and many more subtle causes. Even the best-intentioned programs were found to foster biases, so, again, an entire industry emerged for humans to examine every conceivable AI output for unintended bias before any steps were taken for implementation. Just as with cyberethical inputs, this increased the demand for a broad societal discourse and examination around what should be the agreed values for identifying and correcting outputs, whether they be racial, socioeconomic, ableist, gender-related, or any number of other values around which we have built a solid consensus to avoid bias over the past decade. And that, too, has led us to embrace THAMES in all K–12 curricula."

"Fascinating," Rumple says.

"Another part of the CEOA field that is really exploding today is the specialty around unintended consequences. As our AI has become ever more powerful and generalized, it's designing everything from new nanomaterials to new traffic patterns. What we've found is that there are sometimes unintended consequences—especially social costs—that fall outside the parameters of the bot to consider. The bots can pretty easily be programmed to catch potential pollution or similarly technical consequences, but there are other areas at which they still don't do a particularly good job. These are usually human values like the social implications of diverting a road or building a new research campus in a neighborhood. The algorithm might correctly recognize that a new roadway would facilitate more efficient traffic flow, but it takes a human to recognize that doing so might deleteriously disrupt a strong, cohesive neighborhood community in a city."

"That makes sense," Rumple agrees.

"But it can also be the task of people just to catch dumb outcomes that result from bad programming—such as making sure an AI factory system doesn't try to produce an infinite number of paperclips.[25] So we've created artificial interruptions in the production chain of even relatively minor or seemingly innocuous tasks to insert a human decision point between the bot's solution plan and the implementation of that proposal. There are now large numbers of people working in jobs where they scour algorithmic outputs for unintended social consequences before the bots then take them to the application stage. These workers need a combination of technical and social analytical skills."

Rumple chuckles softly.

"What's so funny?" Bellamy asks.

"As you're talking all I can think of is that Frederik Pohl quote I've always loved: 'A good science fiction story should be able to predict not the automobile but the traffic jam.'"

Bellamy smiles broadly. "I must get a tattoo of that," she says. They both laugh.

7 DON'T TELL ME WHAT YOU WANT TO BE WHEN YOU GROW UP

The first time Kinzie Farmer met Shawn Cornally, he asked her a question she never expected to hear from a teacher.

It was the fall of 2013. Farmer, then 16 and a rising junior at Prairie High School, a large, comprehensive school in Cedar Rapids, Iowa, had met Cornally while investigating a new program called Iowa BIG. Despite its name, at the time it was actually quite small, with virtually no students. And it was, she soon saw, the opposite of her high school in nearly every way. Iowa BIG was nontraditional, its offerings personalized—Farmer's eastern Iowa school district and two others had created it as a kind of regional co-op to help young people navigate the perils of high school and to increase graduation rates.

Cornally, a science teacher, was one of its cofounders, and when he met Farmer, he asked her: "What makes you angry?"

She thought the question was an odd one, especially coming from an adult. But five years later she can still remember that she had no trouble delivering an instant answer: she was angry about how boys at school treated girls.

"I told him that it pissed me off when I walked in the hallway and saw girls following their boyfriends around who I knew were not treating them very well," she says. "And they would just let them call the shots—which is a very complicated thing to be mad at now, looking back. But at the time I was like, 'That really pisses me off.' So, we kind of dove into that."[1]

Farmer became one of Iowa BIG's first students, driving to the facility each afternoon once most of her school day was done. At first she didn't even receive credit for the work she was doing there, but after a few months the tail quietly began to wag the schoolhouse dog. She basically checked out of her old high school, showing up there, reluctantly, at 8 a.m. for just two classes, Spanish and band ("I was in the drum line," she says). Then she'd spend the rest of her day at the school everyone now simply calls BIG.

Classmates back at Prairie High would ask, "Do you still *go* here?" and the answer was *It's complicated*. Officially she was still enrolled at her old high school, but her mind and her heart began to pull away.

A model student her whole life, by sophomore year Farmer had already figured out her future: "I wanted to go to Notre Dame, Stanford, *yadda yadda*," she says. "'Insert 'Amazing School' here.'"

Like many students, she craved the spotlight that came from big academic feats: taking as many AP classes as possible, graduating at the top of her class (oh, and she'd be class president). "But I think BIG made me realize there were way cooler things that I could do that other people hadn't."

Star student or not, until that point, Farmer recalls, her career at Prairie High had also been marked by an odd and persistent lack of trust from adults, one that literally trickled down to the smallest, most elemental detail of life: hydration. "We couldn't have a water bottle with us because there was the threat of it being filled with alcohol," she says. "So, I couldn't carry a water bottle, my backpack, or a snack to class, let alone my phone—I couldn't even have it in the hallway."

By contrast, her teachers at BIG didn't much bother with her water bottle. That was, in a way, the point. They had bigger concerns.

During her junior year, and with Cornally's help, Farmer channeled her anger into the germ of an idea: a way to empower girls to stand up for themselves. This eventually took the form of a one-day conference called Success^she ("Success to the power of she"). It featured six speakers that Farmer had researched, tracked down, pestered, and persuaded to speak, including Lisa Bluder, the head coach of the University of Iowa's women's basketball team, and Kimberly Reynolds, at the time Iowa's lieutenant governor. Reynolds has since been elected governor.

Farmer can still, without notes, remember the date: May 9, 2014. The event was small—only about 150 people attended— but it knocked something loose. "It's the most incredible feeling to have someone trust you and then to be able to show up and produce something," she says.

After the success of the conference, Farmer could feel herself pulling away from Prairie High. While the neighborhood high school held less interest, the work required to conceive and pull off the conference had actually brought her closer to her little eastern Iowa city itself. "I started having more roots in Cedar Rapids," she says. "I identified as a community member—and an Iowa BIG student."

Five years later and speaking by phone 1,500 miles away—by 2019 she was a senior at Gonzaga University in Spokane, Washington—Farmer could still vividly recall the teachers and mentors who trusted her to do something, well, big back in Iowa. She could still access that feeling: "I easily can get emotional about this," she says. "To be given this freedom was like, 'OK: I will do *anything* to keep this.'"[2]

To be fair, most schools hand students this kind of freedom all the time, but it is often handed out unwittingly. The reason we rarely notice it is because it typically kicks into gear after school lets out, in the late afternoon or early evening. It is embodied in projects, but they are seldom called projects: the grand collective effort that goes into producing the weekly school newspaper, mounting the spring musical, or winning the statewide debate competition. It is the effort that goes into being ready and able to face down a crosstown rival on the basketball court or football field. It often consumes large swaths of the emotional life of a school, yet it is almost always relegated to the "extracurricular" hours that take place after the last bell rings.

"There are many parts on the perimeter of what happens in school that are true project-based work, that empower kids to take leadership roles and do real work," says educator Ron Berger. "We just put them on the margins of school rather than the center."[3]

It is that effort, that deadline-based, audience-focused problem solving, that defines the kind of change our schools will likely need over the next generation. Unfortunately, Berger and others say, project-based learning arrives with a bit of baggage. Projects themselves have a long, "spotty" history.

"The word 'project' alarms a lot of educators as being less than rigorous or something that distracts from real, hard, and deep academics. And that nervousness, or that skepticism on the part of educators is warranted." It's the right response, he says, because many teachers have, unfortunately, reduced projects to lackluster schemes amounting to an assigned diorama or poster board to convey student understanding of obligatory classroom readings. "It's not necessarily pushing either their thinking about literature and understanding of literature, or their craftsmanship, necessarily, in the medium that they're working in."[4]

Berger, who runs Massachusetts-based EL Learning (the "EL" once stood for "Expeditionary Learning"), visits hundreds of schools a year. "When a school tells me, 'We're doing a lot of project-based learning,' I'm happy to hear it, but not ready to commit to being excited until I actually see the quality of what kids are doing. There really is a danger that if people are doing projects, that they're doing lightweight work." But if schools take them seriously, he says, "you realize that the way real life works is *all* projects."

Educator Jaime Casap, whose work has been instrumental among educators pushing to do more—and better—project-based education, says he talks to thousands of high school students each year. Yet Casap, who cofounded a public high school in Phoenix built around computer science, never asks students: *What do you want to be when you grow up?* Instead he asks: *What problems do you want to solve?*

Then he asks: *How do you want to solve these problems? What do you need to know? What do you need to be able to do?* And finally: *What do you need to learn?*[5]

"I'm always intrigued by traditional schools' mission statements," says Trace Pickering, who, along with Cornally, cofounded BIG in 2013. The statements, he says, "tend to always be future-focused—'getting kids future-ready—getting kids all this.' I'm clearly not opposed to that, but it implicitly ignores the fact that they're human beings *now* who can be making contributions to their community now. It's not some future state that we hope they attain. We're very focused on: *How can you be a fully self-actualized human being now, who can contribute and not have to wait until you're twenty-two?*[6]

The projects that BIG students end up working on, Pickering said, are "rich, meaty, academic, meaningful" projects that community partners want done. Mostly they're local companies, nonprofits, or government agencies, and mostly the projects aren't "mission-critical." These are teenagers, after all, he says. "They're going to screw it up. It's going to take longer for them to figure it out. But what we also find is that, oftentimes, the solutions they find are something that the companies would have never come to."

So when a camp for physically and mentally disabled children presented BIG students with a four-acre parcel and said that it wanted to turn it into "some kind of experience for our campers," Pickering's students set about creating a solar- and wind-powered garden with wheelchair-accessible raised vegetable beds, fashioned out of concrete. A local contractor agreed to manufacture the beds for free if it could retain the patent for the design. The camp, for its part, said the garden idea, while not quite what they had in mind, was on an entirely different level than what it had been considering.

What's often missing in most education is not content but context, says Pickering. So, for instance, if they're teaching public speaking, most high schools would teach the content and have students try it out on classmates. BIG goes one step further, dropping speakers into enemy territory. "There's a huge difference between speaking to fifteen people who largely agree with you or 300 people who you're trying to convince, who are skeptical," Pickering says. "Those are completely different contexts, completely different skill sets."[7]

Talk to Pickering for a few minutes and one key word comes up again and again: *real*.

"Everything kids do here is real," he says. "Nothing's made up. There's no fake work to do. Worksheets are fake work. School projects for the teacher are fake work. You have to create a fake context for it."

At BIG, every project is connected to the community—to a business partner, nonprofit, or government agency, with real outcomes and real expectations. "There's a real context to it and that real context demands interdisciplinary understanding."[8]

In one recent project, a local company wanted to figure out why it kept winning the annual "best place to work" award, an honor it wasn't actually trying to win. They had a sense but weren't exactly sure why. So, they offered BIG a contract to develop a companywide survey. The students researched survey methodologies, implicit bias, and how to write effective questions, then wrote and tested trial surveys and administered the real thing. They spent two months performing statistical analysis—many students had arrived at BIG without these skills, Pickering says, and learned them along the way. They eventually presented the findings to the company's board of directors.

The entire project took a year. A paid polling firm, he says, could have knocked it out in eight weeks, but the partners understood: "It's about learning."[9]

Like Farmer, Kyle Duane Kazimour wandered into BIG midway through high school, encouraged by a friend to join this "really weird" program. He asked her to explain it first, but she said, "I can't really explain much—you just need to do it."[10]

Kazimour showed up his junior year and actually learned more about the problems he *didn't* want to solve. He thought he'd like architecture, so he led a project for an architecture firm, but didn't care for the work. An amateur photographer, he happened to mention it to one of his BIG teachers, who asked, "What do you want to do with this?"

Kazimour said he'd someday like to make a documentary film, and the next thing he knew he was driving down to Shueyville, Iowa, about fifteen minutes south of Cedar Rapids, to meet an elderly couple who, in the face of encroaching suburban sprawl, had put a conservation easement on their eighty-three-acre property. Kazimour didn't actually know what a conservation easement was, but he was willing to talk with the couple. After meeting them, he thought to himself that if they cared that much about the land in the face of generous offers to sell it, there must be something special here. He thought, *I want to understand why this is special.*

Soon he was setting up interviews, writing scripts, and planning shoots. "The way that they opened up to us about their entire lives—it just seemed like what we were doing was very real."

Kazimour eventually led a nine-person team that created "Somewhere Only We Know," a documentary short.[11] In the bargain, he became a conservation activist in spite of himself. "I didn't even know that I cared about this kind of stuff," he says.

Kazimour graduated in 2018 and began an internship at BIG, running its social media feeds and shooting promotional videos. He also moved out of Cedar Rapids, about twenty minutes south, to a town called North Liberty, about halfway to Iowa City. By the time he turned eighteen, he says, Cedar Rapids had become "this weird safety net" that was holding him back. He remembers thinking to himself, "I feel very, very supported by everyone, but wow, I am not being challenged.'"[12]

When most students show up for the first time at Iowa BIG, Pickering said, "They don't know how to manage their time because they're told where to be, what to do, every second of the day at school—when they can take a piss, when their class is over, when they're going to eat lunch—all that stuff. They're told where to be at all times and they're told what to learn in the order the adults want."

The school, he says, has to "strip all that away if you want to give a person efficacy and ownership." In a way, it offers a kind of unschooling, in which students are constantly asked if they're using their time wisely, if they're accomplishing what they set out to do.

In a way, he says, the school "recultures" them, teaching them to not just take charge of their learning but to accept the successes and failures that come with it. A psychologist might say they're shifting from becoming extrinsic to intrinsic learners. Actually, Pickering says, it goes further than that. "This sounds more craft than it really is, but we *do not care* if projects are successful or not. We just don't care, because in real life, a lot of projects aren't successful. Learning happens whether the project is successful or not, and in fact often more learning occurs when a kid's project crumbles and falls."

In case it's not entirely clear, he adds: "All we care about is the learning."[13]

Farmer, who at sixteen arranged the conference to empower women, felt what it was like to fail perhaps better than anything else. Once she'd decided to create the conference, she applied for a license to slap the coveted "TEDx" label on it— she spent weeks on the application and sent it in, then waited. Weeks turned to months, and even as she began to wonder whether the TED folks would eventually sign off, she and her classmates realized they'd begun telling everyone that it was happening. "All of the speakers were kind of sold on coming and doing 'TEDx Iowa BIG' or 'TEDx Cedar Rapids,'" she recalls.

One day, Cornally casually suggested that Farmer check in on the license. She called TED and waited while the receptionist put her on hold, then got back on the line and said, "It was declined the day you sent it in."

Rejected by TED.

Farmer was crushed. "I mean, as a student who never got less than an 'A' in high school, I was just like, 'Shawn, this is never going to work. We've got to do something else.'"

A lot of the feeling of failure, she says, was "the sucker-punch of 'You are sixteen and you can do nothing basically. You're a kid,'" she says, "even though they probably didn't even know my age when they declined the application. And Shawn, an adult who had so much riding on the success of Kinzie Farmer and the project, basically, looked at me and was like, 'No, we're going to do something and it's going to be awesome.'" And, she informs an interviewer, it was.

The following year, as a senior, Farmer did it again, leading a team of a dozen students that started a movement called "Gussie Down"—it challenged women to go a week without makeup and post pictures on social media. The group also hosted a shark tank event for middle school girls, called "Minnow Tank."

She has since interned in Governor Reynolds's office—the governor-elect invited Farmer to her inauguration in 2019, but Farmer was in class at Gonzaga, studying marketing and minoring in Spanish and leadership. "She still keeps in touch like that," Farmer says. "That's so crazy to me."

Farmer often thinks back to her high school years and longs for the feeling of "doing something that mattered, doing something that was different from everyone else, because I had it for two years—in high school." Reached in March 2019, she said she was most excited for a summer internship at a tiny tech start-up in Coeur d'Alene, Idaho. "Really, I think, Iowa BIG created this desire to be in uncharted territory."[14]

THE THREE Cs: CARING

As they walk, Rumple says, "This whole field of cybercurating appears to employ vast numbers of people in jobs that didn't even exist twenty years ago. It makes me think of similar changes I've seen, like the job of web designer that my nephew held at the time I began to doze. That certainly didn't exist when I graduated from high school in 1980, because there was no web to design."

"A good analogy," Bellamy says. "Actually, the numbers in the cybercurating industry today are far greater than the total working in the web industry even fifteen years ago. And it has completely penetrated every corner of the globe."

"So, most people today work in some sort of cybercurating job?"

"Actually, no," Bellamy corrects. "Remember, today's economy is marked by Three Cs: creating, cybercurating, and caring sectors. The caring sector is by far the largest of the three, much larger even than the other two combined."

Wrinkling his nose somewhat, Rumple says, "I have to confess that the image that immediately conjures for me is of millions of people working in drudgery with low-paying health profession jobs like nursing aides."

"Most of that sort of thing is handled by robots now," Bellamy clarifies. "But there are innumerable ways in which people can work in the caring sector. There are so many things people can do to support others. Robots might take care of menial physical needs in the health industry, but there is always a place for caring professionals to support, encourage, and assist patients and families going through medical treatments. We've also found something very interesting and unexpected take hold in the medical and health fields: as AI has grown more generalized and sophisticated, machine programs have surpassed the best humans as medical diagnosticians. This has resulted in a partial displacement of physicians at the forefront of diagnosing patient illnesses, but it has been a net boon for public health worldwide as well as for employment in medicine—though admittedly requiring some key adjustments in training."

Rumple interrupts her. "I find it a bit hard to believe that people would trust and be satisfied with a robot doctor."

"Well, you're partly correct," Bellamy says, "but it's a bit more nuanced than that. While people were initially resistant to trusting the diagnosis provided by a bot, over time, as the evidence mounted about the comparative advantages in accuracy and in the sheer capacity of the program to scan for every conceivable pattern in patients' symptoms, most people began to insist that their doctors run an AI analysis of whatever ailed them. Since no additional human input was required, the cost approached zero. It wasn't long before it became clear that the best outcomes actually came from having a highly trained clinician collaborating with the bots on patient diagnostics. But that required far fewer diagnosticians—one human doctor could now handle a great deal more patients when AI ran most of the diagnostics. There was a lot of talk that the profession would be decimated."

"I can only imagine," Rumple says.

"Then the really interesting part came in. Back when human physicians ran the system, the best clinical practitioners on the planet were very few in number, a handful of doctors who tended to be highly concentrated in expensive regions and accessible to only a small percentage of the population—typically the most affluent, of course. Since bots have become the preeminent diagnosticians, effectively all nine billion people on the planet have direct access to the best diagnostics available in the world, at little to no cost. The benefits to global health have been immense."

"Nine billion?" Rumple asks.

"You've been asleep for a while," Bellamy says with a smile. "Another interesting thing that emerged was that, as you say, people for the most part just do not want to have a cold machine tell them they have a serious illness—or to tell them what their course for recovery will be. That has led to an entire cadre of medical practitioners who help interpret an AI program's diagnosis, explain it to patients, and help guide them with empathy and human warmth through the course of treatment. These practitioners don't need the immense clinical content training previously required of physicians, but they understand enough to be a compassionate and informed human intermediary between the bot and the patient."[15]

"Shifting from content fluency to content literacy and process fluency," Rumple murmurs thoughtfully, stroking his chin.

"Sound familiar? You're getting it! Exactly! And, what's more, now medical schools have different selection criteria, and they have shifted the way they train students. Today, one of the key qualifying traits for med school admission is an innate and demonstrable capacity for empathy. The curriculum in medical school now places strong emphasis upon further enhancing those medical students' empathic skills, so that they can become optimal caring medical intermediaries."

"Empathy or bedside manner sure wasn't a hallmark of most doctors in my experience," Rumple says.

"How could it be," Bellamy asks, "when the urgent and almost exclusive need was to train doctors up to the highest possible content competency?"

"So, let me get this straight," Rumple intones. "Every person on the planet now has direct access to the best medical diagnosis in the world, and, as they go through treatment, they interact closely with a compassionate medical professional who has been selected and trained for high empathic competency?"

"That's about the size of it," Bellamy nods.

"It sounds like you've built a medical paradise!" Rumple exclaims.

"Well, it's not perfect, by any means, but it has resulted in a tremendous upsurge in every metric of global health. And we've been able to ensure full employment in the caring fields, of which medicine is just one."

"But don't humans make any of the higher-tier intellectual contributions to medicine anymore?" Rumple asks, ruefully.

"Oh, certainly," Bellamy rejoins. "That hasn't gone away by any means. It just isn't the dominant paradigm, and the roles have evolved. Cutting-edge medical research is conducted today by a combination of human biologists and AI systems collaborating closely. The biologists are essential on so many levels, including imaginative leaps or gut hunches that only humans can experience, but also in determining the values and goals that shape the R&D.

"What's more," she continues, "we still have highly trained specialists who look over lab images and biopsy results, but their job has changed quite a bit. Twenty years ago, they typically would have been looking over hundreds and hundreds of results, which was a bit mind-numbing and not a very efficient use of their training. Now, bots do a much better job than humans at scanning through medical imagery for any anomalies. It's only the ones that the bots flag as potential concerns that are then carefully perused by the humans. These specialists are now actually called 'exceptions managers' in medical parlance.[16] The algorithms highlight the lab images that they have identified for further scrutiny, and then the specialized human practitioners apply all of their skills just to those images, in collaboration with the bot, to arrive at a diagnosis."

Rumple pauses to take this in, then surmises: "I imagine people still want their mental health counselors to be humans."

"The answer to that will probably surprise you, because it has surprised most of us," Bellamy responds. "It turns out that a significant number of people actually prefer a counseling bot to a human counselor. Not everyone, to be sure. Some still prefer a person, while others prefer a blended approach of bot and breathing counselor. But between a third and a half of people actually feel more comfortable with the objectivity and, well, the machine mind of the counseling bot; it turns out that many patients harbor suspicions that a human psychologist is secretly judging them."

"Hmm, I could see that," says Rumple.

Bellamy nods. "The medical field is just one example of a profession being disrupted and then reconstituted, often in unexpected ways, but generally with enhanced outcomes for people's well-being. There have also been many jobs created in the social services and community nonprofit sectors."

"How did that happen?"

"As productivity soared, governments began to create more publicly funded jobs to ensure that all able people had gainful employment. This was also good for the economy, because it guaranteed that there were enough consumers to keep the financial wheels spinning. As a country, we had reached the point where machines could provide everyone's material needs and most services without putting every person to work. So, we gravitated toward government funding in the service of putting people to work, providing services that brought the human touch: more teachers and smaller classrooms, more social workers, more community service organizations, generally. There seems to be no limit to how many ways people can help people, so the need appears inexhaustible. And there is pretty strong evidence that these increases in education and social service employment have led to a direct lowering of dropout rates, crime, and other social concerns. And just as with the curricular changes in medical schools, this rapid increase in the caring professions has generated a dramatic emphasis on empathy and compassion in the K–12 curriculum."

"So, the Three Cs economy has had a profound impact on education," Rumple muses.

"Actually, some people refer to the 'Three Cs curriculum' as a direct corollary to the Three Cs economy: the creativity, caring, and collaboration curriculum, where collaboration means human-to-human as well as human-to-bot collaboration. Some of the human collaboration would be familiar to you, but some of it might be new. For instance, as you've seen, beginning in second grade and continuing throughout their subsequent education, students are expected to make a regular habit of crowdsourcing most of the design challenges they're given in school—not just with other students in the school, but globally, with students and even experts around the world. And they do that with increasing sophistication as they progress through the grades. Then they're expected to collaborate with bots to see patterns in the data, make sense of it, and develop a comprehensive narrative, replete with infographics, of their results. This prepares them quite well for idea generation and design in the new workplace."

"What you're describing," Rumple exclaims, "is, in some ways, a very heartening outcome to the challenges I remember we were facing on the cusp of these new technologies, but, in other ways, it is a brave new world."

"Well," Bellamy says, "Huxley used that phrase to refer to a cautionary dystopia but remember that Shakespeare placed those words on the lips of Miranda as an expression of wonderment and delight."

Rumple nods. "That's true."

"Come, let me show you another classroom . . ."

8   THE PYRAMIDS ARE CLOSED FOR REVOLUTION

In the spring of 2013, as educators at the Democracy Prep urban charter school were planning one of their first trips to South Africa, they struck upon a bit of good fortune: they could buy cheaper tickets if the trip from New York's John F. Kennedy International Airport included a fifteen-hour layover in Cairo.

They took it as a sign—the students could see another world capital on their way to Johannesburg and the school could pay less for the privilege. They purchased the tickets and told everyone the good news.

On July 2, 2013, a group of just-graduated Democracy Prep Charter High School students departed from JFK. After a long overnight flight, they arrived the following morning in Cairo. As they walked through the terminal on their way to a waiting charter bus, chaperones and students noticed that their fellow passengers were all gathered around TV monitors. After a while they stopped and took in what was on the screens: scenes of celebration in the streets of Cairo, just outside the terminal. While they'd slept aboard their overnight flight from New York, military leaders had deposed Egyptian

President Mohammed Morsi in a coup that one general called a "national reconciliation." General Abdel Fattah el-Sisi said the military had ousted Morsi because he had failed to fulfill "the hope for a national consensus."[1]

Egypt's first democratically elected president, Morsi had also become an object of frustration as critics said he made political decisions that favored Islamists, while doing little to improve the country's struggling economy. The coup sent jubilant Egyptians into the streets.

They weighed their options and gave the students a choice: they could stay in the relative calm and safety of the airport for the day—their connecting flight to Johannesburg was scheduled for that evening—or they could climb aboard the bus, see the city, and watch the protests unfold. Their driver assured them that traveling in the region remained safe, despite the coup.

Seth Andrew, the school's founder, often talks about the importance of what he calls "juxtaposition," of putting students off guard by introducing them to new and challenging situations with just enough discomfort to make the moment memorable—but with just enough of a safety net so they know they'll be fine.

Juxtaposition is at the heart of innovation and creativity, of pretty much everything we want our young people to embody. It's what gives rise to new ideas. And it's nearly the opposite of how AI typically works.

If we are trying to help young people find their way in an increasingly automated world, along with the instructional strategies outlined elsewhere, another promising way to think about effective education, deep learning, and time well spent is to think seriously about working travel into our schools' curricula and cultures. Getting on a bus or plane and visiting someplace halfway around the world is obviously something a robot or machine intelligence could not and would not do. But perhaps more importantly, it is something most Americans would not do—just 42 percent even hold a passport, and that's after three decades of explosive growth.[2] By contrast, 66 percent of Canadians and 76 percent of Britons hold one.[3]

Travel, of course, gives students a way to think about the world and their place in it that can't come any other way. It builds resilience and tests the boundaries of trust by adults in ways that can have a profound impact on students' lives. For low-income kids, travel may be especially beneficial—it levels the social playing field and gives them access to experiences, attitudes, and ambitions that are otherwise reserved for wealthy or middle-class kids.

Travel is expensive, obviously—perhaps even extravagant by most schools' budgetary standards. But just as schools of the past blanched at the extravagance of a desktop computer—or, in an earlier time, of an upright piano—so too may schools of the future will look back on this period and wonder how they ever operated without a robust, embedded, and purposeful travel syllabus.

Perhaps no other schools in the US place a greater emphasis on travel—and rely on it more heavily to teach key lessons—than Democracy Prep. Founded in 2005 with a single middle school in Harlem, the network has grown to more than twenty schools in five states, educating about 6,500 students. The network includes seven high schools—five in New York City and one each in Camden, New Jersey, and Las Vegas.

Younger students at Democracy Prep middle schools take the kinds of trips one would expect, to key historic and cultural sites in places like Boston, Montreal, and Washington, DC. But the network's high school students do something else altogether, essentially auditioning each spring to visit one of four continents, one in each of their four years of high school.

The schools each spring send groups of about twenty students to Italy, Ecuador, South Korea, and South Africa. On occasion, they swap out South Africa for Senegal.

Selection for the middle school travel is based almost exclusively on students' grades and behavior, while for older students it's a little more nuanced. "We intentionally don't take the top students," says Democracy Prep Charter High principal Elisa DiMauro. Grades and behavior matter. "If you're getting sent out every single day and getting suspended every single week, we don't trust you in a foreign country yet," she says. But if you submit a strong application, nail the interview, and have a solid, "maybe not perfect" resumé, you're in a solid position to be chosen as one of the twenty or so students sent to another continent.

In all, about one in six Democracy Prep students goes abroad each spring. "I think it's one of the most important things that we do, honestly," DiMauro says.[4]

Natasha Trivers, Democracy Prep's superintendent, says travel affords students "layered experiences over time." Trivers, who has spent much of her career in Boston working for educator Doug Lemov's Academy of the Pacific Rim, was attracted to Democracy Prep for two reasons: its citizenship curriculum and its commitment to international travel. "It felt very special to me, as someone who grew up in a low-income household and didn't get to travel much myself. It felt so special and unique that a school would figure out how to make international trips happen for a percentage of the student population every year."[5]

The trips obviously give kids exposure to different places and cultures, she says. But they also lend kids "this cultural capital of being world travelers, of being able to walk into a college environment where often Black or Brown low-income students feel like impostors."[6] They can talk not just about seeing world capitals but can engage more fully in discussions

The Pyramids Are Closed for Revolution

about economic and social justice, she says, because they've seen wealth firsthand in South Korea and poverty in Ecuador.

On a more basic level, she says, the trips crystallize students' perceptions of their own world—they come away from the South Africa trip asking how racism there looks different from (or the same as) racism in the United States. How does poverty in Ecuador look compared to poverty in Camden, New Jersey? "I definitely think there is real power in seeing the world up close and seeing how some of the same systems of oppression, or kinds of inequity, how it looks in a different context," Trivers says, "but also how there are striking similarities."[7]

The South Africa trip typically includes homestay visits with families from a private school, which often present students with the discomfort of wealthy white families employing Black servants from surrounding townships. What his students aren't quite ready for, however, is the disorienting experience of witnessing wealthy Black families employing Black servants. "That gave a really difficult cognitive dissonance for our kids, because here you had Black families employing, and in some ways, treating other Black families as second-class citizens in their own homes."

The Ecuador trip is built each spring around service learning, sending tenth graders to work in schools, orphanages, and medical clinics. The idea came to Andrew as he was thinking about college applications. He realized that rich kids routinely put these experiences on their college applications. *Experience: Service learning in Ecuador.* "So, I was like, 'All right: I want my kids to have service learning in Ecuador.'"[8]

Like Andrew, Trivers sees the power in "disruption and discomfort." Invoking the schools' motto—"Work Hard. Go to College. Change the World!"—Trivers asks, not entirely rhetorically, "How are you ever going to change the world if you haven't seen the world?" She says the experience of sleeping in temples in South Korea or sitting on the floor or staying with a host family and eating what's given to you—"and not getting to go to McDonald's"—teaches students to adapt to an uncertain world. "And I think there's great power in that."[9]

Alize-Jazel Smith, a 2013 graduate who was among the students on that Cairo trip, recalls that Andrew had a rule about eating in restaurants while abroad: students couldn't eat American food—period. "It pissed everyone off, because we would drive past a McDonald's or a Popeye's and he'd be like, 'Nope, nope—you have to eat something that's from here.'" Six years later, she confides, "I am now a foodie—I love food. I love all different kinds of foods. I actually don't like eating American foods that often."[10] She attributes much of that to the experiences she had overseas.

But ultimately, Trivers says, the most powerful aspect of travel is the implicit message it sends to students about their basic worth: "You are not constrained by the boundaries of your community—you are not defined by them." Students may bring to the experience a kind of pride in having grown up in Camden or Harlem or West Las Vegas—but visiting far-off places, for all of its difficulties and expenses, is a kind of basic human entitlement. It tells students, "You are powerful enough to travel this world. You deserve to be in any of these places and you're going to be enriched by the experience—but the people who live there will be enriched by you too."[11]

Most Democracy Prep alumni are first-generation college students, and until they get to college, DiMauro says, her students have lived virtually their entire lives—and experienced their entire education—in Harlem, alongside predominantly Black and Brown classmates. "It's all kids that look like them." With the exception of students who go on to attend historically Black colleges or predominantly Hispanic-serving institutions, these students arrive on campuses each fall where most people don't look like them and haven't had the same experiences. Travel, she says, is a kind of equalizer, a universal social currency. Your new Yale roommate may boast that her family summers in France, but you can at least respond, "The day I went to the Eiffel Tower, it was raining."[12]

Or perhaps, last summer, you witnessed a revolution in the streets.

That morning in 2013, two students opted to stay in the airport. The rest ventured into the city.

Smith was one of the students who boarded the bus. She recalls that she wasn't so sure of the wisdom of her decision at the time. "We were like, 'Whoa, is it safe?'" She finally decided that watching and listening were key. "We know that things happen when people are trying to make change. As long as we're not saying anything or doing anything disrespectful or out of the ordinary, and not drawing that much attention to ourselves, we should be fine." She recalls thinking to herself, "'This is their thing. This is their fight. This is their uprising.' So, we're going to let them do their thing."[13]

They'd scheduled a trip to the pyramids, but when they arrived, a sign at the entrance read "Closed." A clerk approached the bus and apologized. "I'm sorry," he told the group, "the pyramids are closed for revolution."

Without a clear itinerary for the rest of the day, they improvised, eventually finding a camel ride concession, among other attractions, along the way.

Smith, who would go on to study physics and computer science in college, made such strong connections with her South African host family that she returned four years later to visit them for a month over Christmas break. "They treat me as if I was their daughter," she says with obvious pride.

A year before her first trip to South Africa, in the fall of 2012, she'd come face-to-face with what it means to be self-reliant, during a harrowing school-sponsored trip to South Korea. She'd successfully auditioned and had a ticket, but had yet to secure her passport—the trip was to take place just a few days after Hurricane Sandy ravaged the East Coast, and Sandy flooded the local passport office, delaying its processing. That meant she couldn't leave the United States. Her group flew away and left her behind.

Through a bit of good fortune and persistent harassment from the school, Smith's passport arrived the following day and she somehow got on the next flight from JFK to Seoul—with a catch: she had to navigate a layover and plane change in Tokyo. She was seventeen and had never flown internationally. Actually, it was only the second time she'd ever been on an airplane.

Smith arrived in Tokyo and began searching for her connection. After a bewildering fifteen minutes wandering around the terminal—she'd learned Korean at Democracy Prep, but not Japanese or Mandarin—she finally figured out how to interpret the signage and made her way to the proper terminal, then the proper gate, for her flight to Seoul. She made it to Korea to cheers from her fellow travelers.

She jokes that traveling when you're in high school, "while you're still so young and still don't know much," is actually more impactful than the kind of traveling most adults do. "I mean, it's good either way, but I think when people travel, usually they travel to go on vacation. They don't say, 'I'm going to go to the Bahamas and then go to the museums, try to learn about the culture.' Everyone's like, 'I'm going to the Bahamas, I'm going to the beach where the sand is pink, and then take a bunch of pictures.' But I think it was very important and unique for them to say, 'I'm going to take you guys across the country and to go abroad, but we're not just going to be on vacation. We're going to actually learn about where you are.'"[14]

The trips changed everything for Smith; they taught her about bias, for one thing—hers and others'—and about the importance of trying to understand the choices and attitudes of people in different places. "It kind of made me more of a well-rounded person," she says.

But the trips, and the trust that adults had placed in her, also gave her a sense of her own power to make decisions that matter. That strength would guide her, years later, when she decided she had to leave her small Pennsylvania college after she saw troubling signs of racism on campus—including a blackface incident and what she considered inappropriate discipline for a fellow African American student, a football player who knelt during the playing of the national anthem at a football game. She had also vowed to herself that she would someday live someplace where the sun shone more frequently and where the weather was warmer. She breathed deeply, applied to Cal State San Bernardino, and never looked back.

That fearlessness, she says, was always there, hiding. "I think it was part of my personality—I just didn't know it."[15]

RUMPLE VISITS MATH CLASS

Rounding the corner of an upper-floor corridor, Bellamy warns Rumple, "This next class may rattle you. Mr. Conrad does things differently."

Rumple, hearing this, laughs. "Many of my best teachers were divergent thinkers," he says. "I am quite comfortable with risk taking."

Bellamy raises her eyebrows, stops at their destination, and grasps the doorknob. "Good—then you won't be disappointed."

The door opens on a raucous classroom scene, with a multi-tiaged group of students chattering animatedly, focused on the image of a computer screen projected to fill an entire wall at the front of the classroom. "Quiet, everyone—quiet!" the teacher says, holding up a hand. The class settles down as he walks over to a table occupied by a small group of younger students. He stands over one of its members. The student, staring intently at his own computer screen, seems unsure of what to do, so the teacher leans forward and points at the screen, giving him softly spoken directions as two tablemates look on and the rest of the class waits silently.

Bellamy clears her throat. "Good morning, Mr. Conrad," she says. The entire class turns around at the sound. Conrad, noticing the visitors, looks over. "Hello, Principal Bellamy. Thanks for coming. We were just now taking a break from our statistics lesson."

"Can you tell our visitor a bit about the lesson, please?"

"Of course," he says. "My students are all avid video gamers, so I assigned them each to play a level of their favorite game at home. Then they bring the raw data set to class and analyze their performance."

"That's brilliant," Rumple says. "But how on earth do you extract the gameplay data from their gaming consoles?"

A few students giggle shyly, and Conrad shushes them. "The games all allow players to review how they did in any given level—how many kills they made, how much loot they collected, how quickly they completed the level—that's half the fun," he says. "Most games these days also allow players to download their data into a spreadsheet or other program and analyze it, as you would a sports box score or a Wall Street stock page. Players then have the choice of sharing it online with other players, automatically ranking themselves compared to others. Over the past few years, it has become as important a product for players as the game itself."

"Fascinating," Rumple says.

"One of the things I like best about it is, frankly, how obvious it all is. The data are plentiful and rich. It's naturally personalized, of course—only the player herself has played that particular level in exactly that way. And it is, by definition, of great personal interest to each student since all of them want badly to improve their performance. When I did this with a class last year, virtually all of my students decided to focus their attention on a certain advanced level of a very difficult game. So many of them wanted to find out why they did so poorly. When they analyzed the data, they found that, at a certain point, the level was nearly impossible to beat. They wrote up their results in a paper—it had seventeen authors!—and sent it to the game's publisher, which subsequently tweaked the software to make the game fairer to players."

"Amazing!" Rumple says.

"It has set off a kind of competition among subsequent classes to make as big a splash," says Conrad. "The work is hard, but everyone contributes because they all literally have a stake in the outcome. We're taking a little break this afternoon."

"What are you up to?" Bellamy asks.

"Oh, well, we're having some fun with a bit of applied math from an old online tool I used to play with in college. I've adapted it for the classroom. Give us a moment, would you?"

The guests wait as Conrad guides the boy, who types something into the computer, then looks up at him. Conrad nods and the boy, staring intently at the screen, presses Enter. At that moment, the entire class, which had turned to the image on the wall, explodes in laughter.

"I'm sorry, Henry," Conrad tells the boy over the din. "You've had a bit too much today. You'll need"—he looks at the screen—"two hours to sleep it off." Henry smiles, blushing as his tablemates pat him reassuringly on the back.

Rumple, wondering what the commotion is about, cranes his neck and reads the screen. "Good lord!" he says a moment later. "What is going on here?"

In bold type at the top of the screen he reads the question: *Am I drunk?* Beneath it, in red, the word *YES* blinks accusingly.

Conrad walks over to meet the visitors, extending a hand to Rumple as the principal introduces him as "an old friend who is getting a crash course in recent educational history."

"Pleased to meet you," Conrad says. "I hope you don't mind our little exercise. When we gathered this morning, a few students said they were curious about variables, and I thought this would be fun to play around with."

"'Am I drunk?'" Rumple asks. "That seems an inappropriate question to ask high school students."

"It's a perfectly appropriate mathematical question, my man, and a sound one."

"Not for children!" Rumple shouts back.

Bellamy interjects: "My friend isn't familiar with a few of the recent societal changes we've experienced around things like alcohol." She turns to Rumple. "With the widespread shift to self-driving cars, the conversation around teenagers and alcohol consumption shifted, as well. Parents didn't need to worry about their children dying in car crashes, so they could think more broadly about the biological risks of alcohol. There's no use hiding the fact that teens drink and always have. And, of course, their brains are still developing the ability to make long-term plans and crucial decisions. That's a given. But now we expect young people to look out for one another, to think more critically about the costs of their alcohol consumption, and to responsibly integrate drinking, if it's appropriate, into their family life. It doesn't hurt that we now have tools that can help them visualize the toll that excessive consumption takes on their bodies."

"Why am I not surprised?" Rumple asks.

Bellamy utters a little laugh. "It's our job to help get them up to speed on what's happening in their bodies when they drink. The more data, the better. Mr. Conrad, where did this calculator come from?"

"Ah, it's from one of my mathematical heroes growing up," he says, then turns to the student who had been typing earlier. "Henry, can you explain what's going on here?"

Henry, wide-eyed for a moment, gathers himself up and says, "As you can see from the fields on the screen, deriving blood alcohol level is a fairly straightforward calculation. It also follows a predictable path. It's simply a percentage of ethanol in the blood—in most jurisdictions, the legal limit of drunkenness is defined as 0.08 percent. To get the percentage, one needs input from just four variables: the subject's sex and weight, the amount of alcohol consumed, and how much time has elapsed. Plug these bits of data into the calculator and anyone can quickly answer this question."[16]

Conrad interjects: "Henry, let's help our guest, Mr. Rumple, find his capacity. He weighs . . ." Conrad looks over at Rumple expectantly, who softly clears his throat.

"Um, about two hundred pounds."

"Very well," says Conrad. "Let's say Mr. Rumple went to a party and drank three drinks in quick succession."

A student yells, "Make it ten!"

A third, more politely, suggests: "Make it six."

"Very well," Conrad says. "Six drinks." The students quickly shift their eyes to the screen. Henry, with the help of a table-mate, types in the appropriate numbers.

"What do you think, class?" the teacher asks. "Will Mr. Rumple be drunk?"

They return in unison, "Yes!"

"That's obvious," Conrad replies. "But *for how long*? For how many hours, class?"

Students begin shouting: *One hour . . . two hours . . . six hours*. Conrad signals to Henry, who pushes Enter. "Four hours!" the class says in unison.

"All right, all right," Conrad says. "What would have happened if Mr. Rumple here had taken it a bit easier and had just four drinks?"

One student raises her hand: "Isn't it basically just a straight mathematical function?"

Conrad lets the question hang in the air as Henry, now getting the hang of the tool, quickly types and returns an answer: Rumple would be sober in an hour and a half. From somewhere in the classroom, a lone student exclaims, "Whoa."

"Exactly," Conrad says. "Just a small reduction in consumption makes a huge difference, it seems. So . . ." He looks at his watch. "Play around with the calculator and we'll come together again in a few more minutes. There's a scale in the corner if you've forgotten how much you weigh."

Conrad approaches the group of visitors as Rumple blinks at the screen. "Well," Rumple says, "I guess it's really not such a bad word problem."

"It's far better than most of what appeared in the math text-books of my youth," Conrad replies. "And it gets closer to the essence of what math really is: a way for people to pose inter-esting questions and derive satisfying, useful answers relevant to their lives."

At this, Bellamy chimes in. "Mr. Rumple and I were talk-ing earlier about how, for most students of the past, math amounted to little more than an extended exercise in computation—the one part of math that could easily be done better and more flawlessly by a computer."

"Don't get me started," Conrad replies. "In the past, most math classes spent about three-quarters of their time teaching students how to hand-calculate—that was, of course, the hard-est, most tedious part of math. You literally couldn't do any math without it, so it made sense to focus the longest on giv-ing students that essential skill. But with calculators, it quickly became the *easiest* part of math. So why did we continue to spend all that time teaching it? We soon saw that this was time that could be better spent on computational thinking, on applying math to real-world problems."

"Interesting," Rumple says.

"We should be helping students do real work: How to eval-uate loan rates. How to critique statistics spouted by politi-cians. How to manage their own health. How to ask the right questions, actually, and solve big, messy problems. We so sel-dom used to start from the problems they cared about. It was all abstraction, all raw numbers, out of context. Even when we provided context, it was meaningless—two trains leaving the station, all that. The smartest people, as someone once said, were basically those who were the deepest and most organized filing cabinets, who could produce knowledge, like a file, on demand.[17] Actually, 'regurgitation' is the more apt metaphor. Not anymore. Today, it's the opposite—the students who are considered 'smartest' are the ones who have developed the ability to ask the right questions and proceed confidently. Well, I must get back to my students. They seem to be exploring what happens when they ingest massive quantities of alcohol in a short period of time—talk about regurgitation!"

9 *FESTINA LENTE*, OR CHANGE MANAGEMENT AT ROCKY HILL SCHOOL

American educational history is replete with examples—such as the high school reforms of the nineteenth and early twentieth centuries—of the fact that what many today consider schools' fixed canonical essentials are, rather, historically constructed responses to ever-changing social, political, economic, and technological conditions. All of education practice has been socially constructed to meet the needs of a particular historical episteme; this has always been the case and always shall be.

Today, we find ourselves immersed in a vortex of transformational technology and economic inflections that may be unprecedented in their convergent intensity. Consequently, there is a tremendous need for dramatic and bold (while at the same time thoughtful, informed, and considered) exploration of new educational practices to match these revolutions. Specifically, we need highly protean experimentation coupled with deep intellectual humility to foster a multiplicity of new teaching paradigms that inform an emergent set of classroom practices to speak meaningfully to the needs of children in the dawning digital age of AI and robotics.

Jim's career has been largely predicated on precisely these concerns. His doctoral work in history, which focused on the Black freedom struggles and antiwar movements in the United States from 1940 to 1970, was driven by a desire to understand how morally informed social transformation transpires in concrete social processes and structures. Beginning in about 1999, Jim became convinced that the key factors and challenges for change in our lives today were principally being driven by the digital revolution, which promised to disrupt manifold dimensions of human life and identity at least as deeply as had the Neolithic and Industrial Revolutions, but in a radically condensed timespan of mere decades. He saw that education, which has historically lagged behind many other fields in responding to change, needed now more than ever to get ahead of this curve in order to provide meaningful preparation for future employment and citizenship in a radically altered world. Jim determined to become a school leader in an attempt to straddle theory and practice. This vision informed everything he subsequently did in universities and as the head of a series of private schools.

In 2015, Jim was casting about for a school that was culturally and otherwise well positioned and inclined toward adroitly exploring brave new models for education practice. Experience had taught him that the handful of the most prestigious and well-endowed schools rarely fit this bill, as they tended to be hidebound in tradition and too comfortable to feel any nudge in the direction of risk taking. More likely candidates could be found in the roughly 90 percent of smaller private schools that were hungry to find new ways of surviving and thriving in a rapidly changing world.

Just such a school was Rocky Hill School, which was then looking for a new leader. A pre-K–12 independent school, RHS sits on eighty-four luscious acres along Rhode Island's Narragansett Bay. As it happens, several RHS Board members had previously seen Jim speak about education innovation and had subsequently visited him at one of his previous schools. So, there was already a strong complementarity between Jim's leadership concerns and the RHS board's understanding of what they sought in a new school leader.

The decided majority of independent schools today, with limited endowment, are facing financial challenges from multiple vectors, among them: declining demographics of school-aged children, recent and growing parental demands for new services such as greater learning-difference support that requires a host of new hires, and greatly increased parental expectations for outcomes, most notably that schools will somehow place seniors in the incoming classes of highly selective colleges. The Great Recession of 2008 left in its wake a group of parents who were now more reticent to pay skyrocketing tuition for their children to attend private schools, especially when they live in affluent communities with respectable or even excellent public schools. Even upper middle–class families now expect to be provided with financial aid incentives. These and numerous other challenges have made for strong financial headwinds buffeting every private school.

What separated Rocky Hill from its peers nationwide was threefold: visionary board leadership, a faculty that was both convivial as a community and culturally explorative, and a history of innovation. First, the board was an extraordinarily generative group of trustees engaged with and committed to the school in all appropriate ways. (When Jim's wife asked how the meeting went after his first interview with the board members, Jim replied, "That's a group of trustees with whom I would love to work!") Second, Rocky Hill had an extraordinarily collegial and dynamic faculty who believed in the school, cohered as a community, and were open to emergent practices. Finally, the school had a history of innovation. Years earlier, it had been the first school in Rhode Island to adopt one laptop per child. It had also led its region in adopting the Harkness method of teaching for middle-school and upper-school instruction, further iterating this established method by blending digital tools into the discussions around the tables. These were important elements, as they collectively made for a learning community with innovation in its DNA—and, indeed, that was open to openness.

Jim arrived at Rocky Hill at a time when the school was looking to explore new frontiers while retaining a continuity and internal cohesion with its past. Jim's first step toward a new strategic vision was to define a two-year time horizon for change. Earlier in his career, a wise elder mentor had advised him that, no matter how busy one might be with many demands, the greatest gift one could give a student was one's full attention with "the illusion of infinite time." Jim decided to apply this sage counsel to an entire institution, striving, in a favorite phrase of Caesar Augustus, to foster in the community a spirit of *festina lente*, or hastening slowly, maintaining a steady momentum and even urgency without a frenetic rush to results. He'd portray a calm confidence in the school's future while assuring everyone that they would together create the "most exciting school in Rhode Island."

Jim stipulated that the first of the two years would be committed to what was termed a schoolwide "Vision Quest," while the second year would be committed to beta-testing the implementation of that vision across every dimension of the school. By the beginning of the third year, the RHS collective vision was to be fully launched and embedded in every program across campus. "In two years," he asserted, "someone should be able to randomly parachute anywhere onto campus at any time and unmistakably be able to see us living our vision."

For the Vision Quest, Jim established four parallel committees—one each for faculty, trustees, students, and parents and alumni. Each was provided with three prompts and given three criteria for adoption of ideas.

The three prompts:

1. Imagine, in your mind's eye (i.e., it doesn't have to actually exist), walking into the most important and impactful school on the planet today. What does it look like, and why?

2. What is the next logical evolutionary step for Rocky Hill School in its organic institutional life cycle?

3. How might your answers to 1 and 2 converge here at RHS?

Accordingly, the committees were told that any answer they might develop over the course of the year was allowed, but with the following three conditions for adoption:

1. It must be true to Rocky Hill's DNA.

2. It must be realistic to apply to a K–12 setting.

3. It must be marketable in Rocky Hill's region.

The committees were told that they had a year to explore these prompts and generate new visionary departures for the school.

Significantly, leadership of the process was distributed: an assistant head of school led the faculty committee; a parent led the parents' committee; a teacher led the student committee; and Jim led the trustees' committee—and only the trustees' committee. He attended the various meetings, especially of the faculty committee, but was not a voting member and rarely spoke. That is not to say he was entirely mute throughout the process. Instead, he started a weekly blog to share thoughts about current historical trends and how education might optimally adapt to get ahead of the curve. For those blogs, he sometimes interviewed national thought leaders who, he felt, should be part of the discussion—Tony Wagner,

Susan Fonseca, and Marc Prensky, to name a few. The blog was pushed out weekly to all parents and alumni and posted more broadly. Marc Prensky and Greg Toppo also came to campus to speak about their work in education innovation.

One of the key challenges was helping members of the community who were uncomfortable with extended ambiguity to stay the course through a year of exploration in the "fog of creativity." Some of this entailed empowering those who were engaged by and comfortable with the process to emerge as leaders among peers. Jim also gave all senior administrators a copy of Rob Evans's excellent book, *The Human Side of School Change*, to help everyone stay focused as a leadership team on nurturing, supporting, and encouraging the school's teachers, parents, and students despite the very human discomfort with change and the uncertainty so many felt.

Some members of the community wanted more explicit guidance and even a crisp blueprint from the school head; Jim replied that he could certainly elaborate for them, but only with the guarantee that it would pale in comparison to the richness and brilliance that was sure to emerge from a patient attendance upon the undoubted collective genius of the inclusive community process underway.

Interestingly, even in that first year when the committees were very much in merely germinative mode—in other words, when there had been no material shifts in actual school curricula or programs—a palpable buzz of excitement began to envelop the school. Word went out that it was engaged in daring and bold exploration, that the school was "on the move" toward exciting new initiatives. Word of mouth is particularly important for independent day schools because they predominantly draw from a distinct radius circumscribed by commutable distance. Word of mouth is perhaps more important for Rhode Island day schools than elsewhere, given the small geography and a statewide population only just north of one million.

As early as the fall of that first year, RHS saw dramatic increases in open house attendance, with numbers that had not been attained in years. Even though the changes being considered were not even defined yet, let alone implemented, prospective families anticipated they might be in place by the time their children attended the school.

This uptick continued throughout the year. In fact, admissions applications increased 45 percent year over year, and the school's admissions yield ultimately showed an increase of nearly 20 percent above the previous year—this, in a saturated New England independent school market, at a school that was more than eight decades old. And the newly admitted students were markedly stronger academically as the school was able to become more selective in its admissions process.

This is an important outcome to underscore: initiatives that are at once bold and imaginative tend to enliven the school culture and bolster its word-of-mouth reputation almost immediately, quickly resulting in early wins by even the most traditional of key performance indicators, such as the enrollment funnel and fundraising.

All decent parents want the best for their children, and many translate this concern to the school environment by wanting their children to succeed in the traditional metrics— most saliently, gaining admission to the most prestigious universities so that they can have the greatest possible opportunities at the start of their adult lives. This is understandable and commendable. Over the course of his career, Jim has found that many parents insist upon traditional pedagogies because they fear that any innovation will risk the outcome they desire for their children, especially the "ultimate deliverable" of an Ivy League admission. Lurking behind that fear, however, he has found that most parents today have another—and growing—worry: that the traditional paths are steadily losing their efficacy in delivering success for life. In other words, many parents fear they are setting their children upon an increasingly Procrustean traditional treadmill that is familiar from their own life experience, but that they sense is no longer a correct, certain, or wholesome path to success.

Jim has found that the key to gaining parental support for school innovation is to bring these dual fears to the surface where they can be articulated and examined within the community—and, of equal importance, where they can be both affirmed and critiqued. A large proportion of parents are greatly relieved to find that the cognitive dissonance between what they want for their children and what the traditional path of regurgitative learning, standardized testing, and high-stakes college admissions actually does to and for their children in today's world need not define their families' experience during their children's high school years. Parents who are brought to see that much of success can better be realized today through more innovative paideia often, in fact, become the most enthusiastic supporters of school change. And they bring in many other families by word of mouth—indeed, the many new families clamoring to join always outnumber the comparatively small number who choose to leave due to the innovations.

As spring of the Vision Quest first year approached, the four committees converged on the single word: innovation. It was unanimously recommended by all four committees that RHS become "the most innovative school in Rhode Island." While that may sound a bit vague, it actually engendered considerable clarity in several key ways. For instance, RHS's hiring criteria, program approval process, and resource allocations would now be predicated upon looking for innovation and thought leadership that differentiated the school from its peer competitors. It also gave an unmistakable mandate as an institution to seek out alliances with forces of change and influencers in technology, arts, business, and other sectors in Rhode Island and beyond.

As teachers, administrators, parents, and trustees began to feel the potential of this momentum, there was a growing sense that something distinctive and wonderful was taking place in this community that could have a profound impact on education outside of Rocky Hill's bucolic campus. It was quickly agreed that any innovative programming or pedagogies developed at RHS would be shared with less resourced schools as open-source freeware. In fact, the entire school committed to striving for innovations that were intentionally designed to be scalable and replicable at little or no cost to other schools worldwide. Additionally, any public school in Rhode Island was invited to participate fully, at no cost, in any RHS initiative.

Of course, there was still the challenge of actually building innovation into the warp and woof of the school's fabric. That was the focus of the second year in the Vision Quest. The first step was taken in early July, just after graduation. All teachers were invited to attend a five-day retreat with meetings held six hours per day to share a deep dive into designing realizable, pragmatic initiatives across all grades at the school that incorporated the highest level of innovation. Remarkably, a substantial percentage of the school's teachers attended all thirty hours of the retreat during their well-earned summer vacation.

The engagement was breathtaking. There were moments during those days when Jim sat back, grateful to realize that he was sitting in the most exciting meta-educational discussion he had ever been privileged to experience with peers. RHS teachers were quite clear and articulate about the fact that they were not trying to create something entirely unprecedented. In fact, it was felt that the more they could cull to their purpose from already established models, the less was needed to create *ex nihilo*—from nothing—and, importantly, the more familiar, demonstrated, and acceptable these models would be to teachers and families alike.

It was soon generally agreed that project-based learning (PBL) would be key to programming throughout the entire nursery–12 curriculum. This meant, specifically, a commitment to PBL that, reflecting Marc Prensky's influence, entailed "real-world problem solving." In other words, there would be no "make a terrarium" projects and there would be no purely hypothetical challenges assigned to students. Rather, they would consistently be given challenges such as how to optimize wind energy adoption in Rhode Island or how to apply technology to assist blind people in navigating cities more effectively. In this, the teachers were all inspired by the talk Marc Prensky had given during his visit to the school, in which he cited Zoe Weil's terminology of teaching students to become "solutionaries."

While embracing PBL as the core teaching practice for the school, this was not intended to be to the exclusion of all other teaching modalities. Whenever certain content could most efficiently be imparted by traditional means, those practices were to be retained on an as-needed basis. The key decision was to use PBL as the basis for teaching the "soft skills," or what were alternatively termed "process skills," that RHS felt were essential for future success in a globalized, digitized world of work and endeavor.

To this end, the participants dedicated an extensive, highly collaborative process during that summer retreat to collectively identifying the skills with which they wanted every student to graduate from Rocky Hill School. This institutionally defining list was built up from a broad array of core values that were brainstormed, always with an eye toward two key thematic queries: *What is the quintessence of Rocky Hill School?*

and *What does an exploration of the future of work indicate will be the most important qualities of mind and heart for today's students in a world of AI and robotics?*

At the end of the week, the group unanimously agreed on the following four nouns and four adjectives. Every Rocky Hill student, they agreed, will graduate as

- A Navigator ("You are curious and self-directed, approaching learning with nimbleness, adaptability, perseverance, and resilience.")

- A Critical Thinker ("You ask meaningful questions, develop important knowledge, and use research, analysis, and interpretation to evaluate evidence, arguments, and beliefs.")

- A Citizen ("You are a responsible and engaged member of your community and seek ways to lead and model good citizenship through kindness and respect for others, in physical and digital domains.")

- And a Communicator ("You are a poised and resourceful communicator, able to skillfully express yourself in many modalities for a variety of audiences.")

WHO IS

- Innovative ("You are a bold thinker, generating new and creative ideas and willing to take risks to solve complex problems, individually and as part of a group.")

- Self-Aware ("You are confident in your personal strengths, attentive to your needs, empathetic to others, and honor your health and well-being.")

- Ethical ("You act with honesty, integrity, and a focus on social responsibility.")

- Globally minded ("You value diversity and different perspectives, understand global issues, and approach the world with an open mind.")

In addition to inviting faculty and administrators to the July strategic retreat, students also, importantly, were included, ranging from fifth graders to eleventh graders. They were not included in the faculty discussions, but met separately on campus. They worked as a single team on the following prompt: "'Rocky' (choose Rocky's gender as you wish) is going to be a new kindergartner this year, graduating from twelfth grade in 2030. Describe the ideal 'thick learning experiences' that Rocky will experience in each grade before graduating, if Rocky Hill School were the best, most exciting, and most impactful Rocky Hill you can imagine."

This group had two remarkable teachers assigned to work with them toward the goal of presenting Rocky's journey to all of the adults before the end of the retreat. These teachers spent time discussing with the students what "thick learning experiences" meant, and they facilitated the students' own processes.

The students quickly ascertained that they collectively considered Rocky a girl. They then put together a presentation for their teachers that was remarkably convergent with what the faculty were developing on the other side of the building. They envisaged Rocky pursuing a series of challenges and interests—"white hat hacking" in the fifth grade, for instance, and organizing public support for enlightened state legislation during her secondary years—that reflected passionate pursuits of feasible solutions to real-world challenges each year, successively requiring increasingly sophisticated skill sets in coding, leadership, communication, analysis, and organization.

When the students finished their presentation, the first comment was from a fourth-grade teacher who remarked how strikingly similar the faculty vision of their dream school was to the students' vision. This further emboldened the teachers to proceed in following their Muse. Moreover, it was an opportunity to communicate to parents why the school was pivoting in this new direction; filming the students (with proper permissions) giving their presentation was a compelling way to convey to parents that the desire for these changes came directly from the children themselves, quite as much as from the teacher cadre.

As the retreat broke up for the summer, participants could reflect on a remarkably constructive year at Rocky Hill School. They had collectively taken a school in its ninth decade from, as Jim described it, "an adult cell state" and "teased it back into a pluripotential stem cell state." The school community was now abuzz with dynamic discussion about what educating for the future might look like, word of mouth and applications were dramatically on the rise, fundraising was up, and many felt themselves part of something substantial, with potential import beyond the walls of their particular school. The faculty, parents, and administrators had collaboratively explored the institution's quintessence as a distinctive community of learning, opened themselves to what education needed globally in an age of exponential technologies, and had committed themselves to making a *sui generis* contribution to helping all schools make similar transformations successfully.

The second year, which had been designated as a piloting/beta testing year before a complete, schoolwide curricular roll-out at the beginning of the third year, was marked by several important steps to facilitate this next phase of exploration. In particular, Jim made key hires that brought two women of remarkable talent, experience, energy, networks, and vision. Meg Stowe joined RHS as the new full-time director of innovation to facilitate the interface between internal constituencies and partnering external organizations. Meg had already had a remarkable career as an educator and entrepreneur, founding the successful nonprofit Girls Leadership Collaborative. Upon starting at RHS, she immediately fostered a series of innovative programs with astounding energy. Another significant contribution to the Rocky Hill community came when Susan Fonseca arrived on campus for a week as the first RHS innovator-in-residence. Susan was a globally impactful entrepreneur and thought leader who had been a founding leader of Singularity University at NASA's Ames Research Center in Silicon Valley. She had also founded Women at the Frontier and the enthusiastically named SheWorks!

In addition to meeting with students in all grades and facilitating innovative student projects during her week in residency, RHS arranged for Susan to speak at the Hope Club in Providence to a gathering of influential Rhode Island women leaders about empowering women around the globe. That talk was so successful that an ongoing group of invitees continued to meet under Rocky Hill auspices.

Susan's visit was so exciting that she was named Rocky Hill's permanent innovator-in-residence, working remotely as school innovator from her home in another state. (This flexibility was also a hallmark of taking risks, seizing opportunities, and leveraging a broader vision as a school of innovation.)

An interesting—and emblematic—student-led transformation came out of one of Susan's visits to a third-grade classroom. Susan shared with the students that she was happy to be in Rhode Island for the week, as it afforded her the opportunity to connect with a wonderful young entrepreneur she knew, Hannah Chung. Hannah had cofounded Sproutel, a company that made plush robotics for children who faced medical challenges. Specifically, Susan described one of Sproutel's products, Jerry the Bear, which was designed to be an interactive companion for children with diabetes.

A perspicacious third grader noted incisively that, even with an interactive companion, it would still hurt to receive shots if one had juvenile diabetes. This led Susan to share the work of a friend who had created the product Buzzy the Bee to make shots painless for children. The entire third-grade class quickly concluded that Jerry the Bear must meet Buzzy the Bee and form a partnership.

Soon thereafter, the founders of both products were working with Rocky Hill children on how the two could be combined into one package for children with juvenile diabetes. The third graders were also thrilled that year to watch news videos of "their" Hannah and her Sproutel team winning the Best of CES Award at the 2018 Consumer Electronics Show for their new product, My Special Aflac Duck (designed for children undergoing chemotherapy treatments).

To the delight of the entire RHS campus, Hannah agreed to become Rocky Hill's permanent entrepreneur-in-residence, collaborating with students in grades two through twelve in the development of new Sproutel products.

As innovation took hold across departments, it was soon announced that artists from the jewelry fashion chain ALEX AND ANI would become artists-in-residence for the spring semester, showing students how to craft a viable career pursuing their artistic gifts. A new master plan of the campus also began to be explored that included a proposed sweep of buildings (some already in place to be refurbished, some to be newly built) designated as a future innovation cluster.

Exploration of how these facilities might be used to further educative interplay between the business sector and RHS classrooms led to a particularly bold prototyping initiative: a collaboration Rocky Hill built with edtech start-ups, particularly in partnership with LearnLaunch, the largest edtech incubator and accelerator in Boston (and perhaps the nation), with more than two hundred companies moving through its coworking space in just the first few years since its founding. As the senior advisor to the board of LearnLaunch, Jim was continually struck by how many edtech products went to market with very little classroom vetting—largely because schools worry about the optics of appearing to allow their students to be "guinea pigs" for for-profit start-ups. At the same time, ironically, it was striking that so many educators were calling for new programs to teach children how to be innovators and entrepreneurs, but that so many of the curricula being generated in this area were anemic versions of playing house.

It occurred to Jim one day that there was an opportunity to foster mutual value by framing entrepreneurs in the classroom as a collaborative undertaking. The students and teachers were to be cocreators of product alongside the entrepreneurs.

Accordingly, Rocky Hill partnered with LearnLaunch to invite founders of edtech start-ups to embed in the school's second- through twelfth-grade classrooms. The founders were invited to stay as long as they wished, up to a year, and were invited to join the community every day for lunch, thus affording them opportunity for informal interactions with teachers and students. This provided the entrepreneurs with a test bed for their products, but also provided teachers and students with a real-world, engaging design challenge in which to participate, building products for future classrooms while learning firsthand about entrepreneurship, teamwork, innovation, iteration, resilience, grit, marketing, product design, and many other skills that could set students on the path to success.

The success of this collaboration rested in part upon some of the rules of engagement that were established from the outset: RHS teachers were fully engaged at key stages all along the way, keeping the process transparent to them and inviting their feedback, including canvassing their opinions as to whether to proceed in the collaboration at all. Importantly for faculty enfranchisement, too, every teacher had the freedom to opt out of any programmatic initiative. Specifically, every teacher was granted the freedom to refuse to allow any program into her or his classroom—and to stop allowing access to that classroom at any time. Interestingly, the result was that not a single teacher opted out of any initiative.

The school leaders also gave presentations to parents at various stages as planning proceeded (explaining, for instance, that all entrepreneurs would have to undergo the same background checks as teachers before being allowed on campus) and allowed all parents to opt out of having their children involved in any activities with entrepreneurs on campus. In the end, only a handful of parents placed any limits on entrepreneurs interacting with their children (and those only specified that they were not to meet alone with their children). This near-universal buy-in was directly due to the preservation of teacher and parent agency in the initiative.

Indeed, it was particularly inspiring to see how many teachers became actively and enthusiastically engaged in building curricula around entrepreneurship in order to facilitate contextual thick learning experiences for the students who were collaborating with founders on campus. Taking class time, for instance, to learn and gamify stages and mindsets of entrepreneurial iteration provided students with a much richer context for listening to, engaging with, and reacting to a pitch or product presentation by a start-up founder.

This was evident in the Buzzy the Bee experience. The third graders asked each of the entrepreneurs to share their first prototypes, their most recent polished versions, and also the version of their product that was made when they were feeling like giving up on their start-up; this was because the students had been studying about iteration and grit to help them better understand the entrepreneurs they would be meeting. Contextual curriculum and real-world modeling reinforced each other in thick educational experiences.

All entrepreneurs who came to campus were required to sign an agreement, part of which stipulated their willingness to allow competent students in grades six through twelve to intern with them; as it happened, the mostly young entrepreneurs who came to campus were quite enthusiastic about working with the students and were very generous with their time. This, in turn, fostered a "start-up culture" among the older students on campus, which became infectious—and was tremendously empowering for those students who embraced it. Key to this empowerment, too, was the capacity and commitment of the administration to support new student initiatives enthusiastically and responsively.

One example of such student leadership to come from this process was Rocky Hill's "Hack for Social Good" focused on innovating solutions for global energy needs. This initiative emerged from the enthusiasm of two students who were particularly inspired and encouraged along the way by Susan and Meg.

The hackathon involved students from seven schools (including one in Toronto) and included Jeanette Manfra, US Assistant Secretary for the Office of Cybersecurity and Communications in the Department of Homeland Security, as well as a US Senator and a US Congressman. Interestingly and importantly, this hackathon originated from Rocky Hill students who had been empowered to envision and implement a significant new departure for the school and who met with a receptive faculty and administration (including a new innovation infrastructure and dedicated innovation personnel) who helped shepherd the students' idea into realization.

The story told in this chapter is of a school transformed into a more explorative and leading-edge learning center that places students at the center of the process of discovery and empowers them to become "solutionaries." A few of these elements were already integral to Rocky Hill's culture, while others have been interwoven with the school's distinctive DNA in the past couple of years, but some broadly applicable lessons pertain to all schools: that the path to relevance and twenty-first-century skills is readily available to any school with the imaginative willingness to innovate, at little to no cost; that traditional metrics such as admissions funnels will quickly improve, because increasing numbers of parents in the educational marketplace recognize the need to provide their children with precisely these new skills, experiences, and qualities of mind; that a key factor in successfully leading such school change is to enfranchise one's faculty to lead, question, and own the process; that students will benefit from and run with these opportunities with enthusiasm and more than occasional brilliance; and that all schools have the capacity to demonstrate remarkable plasticity, given a management culture fostering teacher agency and safe zones for innovation.

RUMPLE VISITS HUMANITIES CLASS

As Rumple and Bellamy approach another classroom, they hear laughter coming from inside. "This is an advanced student-led seminar in American history, culture, and literature," says Bellamy, her hand on the doorknob.

"Is that why they're laughing?" Rumple jokes.

Bellamy smiles. "There's no teacher—only students who have studied the great thinkers, poets, musicians, and writers of different eras. I believe they're studying twentieth-century novelists and playwrights, but they jump around a lot, so at this point they could be talking to just about anyone."

"Talking to . . . *what*?"

She smiles. "Brace yourself."

Bellamy opens the door onto a small group of students in a darkened room, sitting at tables arranged in a semicircle, all facing a figure on a raised platform. The setup resembles nothing so much as a small nightclub or theater. A few of the students notice the pair and Bellamy offers a modest wave, but they quickly go back to the lesson, transfixed by a gleaming figure at the front of the room. As Rumple's and Bellamy's eyes adjust to the darkness, they see a transparent but somehow substantial projection of a stout, bearded man, dressed in khakis and a crisp white shirt, addressing the class. The figure's voice is deep, his motions easy and resolute.

As they quietly walk along the edge of the room, Rumple gets a good look at the figure and can't suppress an amazed exclamation. "Is that . . . Hemingway?"

Bellamy shushes him, then whispers: "They're studying his letters. A few years ago, one of our students scanned the text of all the letters—there are *thousands*—into a database. Along with his novels, magazine pieces, and other writings, they form the basis of this tool. Another student gathered digital images of Hemingway at various points in his life and created a series of holographic likenesses. A third found audio of Hemingway reading his stories and created the voice likeness. The software is cheap, and the process took just a few hours. The figure is programmed to listen to questions, then quickly search the database and access text based on what the algorithm determines is an appropriate passage. It will even track where in the room the question comes from and address the questioner directly. It's all quite simple," she concludes. "It doesn't always work perfectly, but when it does it's remarkable."

"A Papa Hemingway chatbot!" Rumple remarks.

Bellamy leads them to a pair of seats at the back of the room. One of the students, meanwhile, addresses the figure: "We've been reading your letters—you're quite prolific. How did you find time to write so many letters while writing books, stories, and articles, too?"

"I write letters because it is fun to get letters back," the holographic Hemingway replies. "But not for posterity. What the hell is posterity anyway? It sounds as though it meant you were on your ass."[1]

The students laugh, then another asks, "I hope this isn't off-topic, but I know that you and James Joyce were friends in Paris. I've just read *Ulysses*. Have you read it? What do you think of Joyce as a writer?"

"*Ulysses*? A most goddamn wonderful book! I got a copy from Sylvia Beach the week it appeared in Paris, in February 1922. I admired Joyce more than any other writer." The holographic Hemingway stops momentarily, as if remembering something. "Joyce used to tell us all that he was perpetually broke, but after the book came out, I saw him and the whole family at Michaud's every night, eating and drinking. Binney and I, we could only afford to go once a week."[2]

Another student: "Tell us about F. Scott Fitzgerald."

The holographic Hemingway pauses, then says, "We met in 1925. He introduced me to Max Perkins, for which I'll always be grateful. But Scott never fulfilled his potential as a writer. I told him so after I read *Tender Is the Night*, his last novel. I liked it—and I didn't. It started off with that marvelous description of Nicole and Dick Diver. Scott based the characters on our friends Sara and Gerald Murphy, but then he started *fooling* with them, making them come from things they didn't come from, changing them into other people." There's a moment of silence as the holographic Hemingway seems to be processing what to say next. He looks up to the ceiling, as if he has decided to address a spirit. "You can't do that, Scott! If you take real people and write about them, you cannot give them other parents than they have—they are *made* by their parents and what happens to them. You cannot make them do anything they would not do. You took liberties with people's pasts and futures that produced not people but damned marvelously faked case histories. You, who can write better than anybody can, who are so lousy with talent that you have to— the hell with it! Scott, for God's sake, write and write truly no matter who or what it hurts, but do not make these silly compromises."

Another student pipes up: "What compromises?"

Hemingway locks eyes with the student: "He stopped listening—except to the answers to his own questions. That's what dries a writer up: not listening. That's why I modeled Harry, the dying writer in *The Snows of Kilimanjaro*, after him. Scott saw it immediately. He didn't like it, but he took it like a man, which I admired."

Another student asks: "Well, what advice would you give Fitzgerald?"

"For Christ sake, write and don't worry about what the boys will say nor whether it will be a masterpiece nor what. I write one page of masterpiece to ninety-one pages of shit—I try to put the shit in the wastebasket."[3]

The students laugh nervously, but the holographic Hemingway paces the floor, seeming like he wants to say more to Fitzgerald's spirit.

"I'd like to see you and talk about things with you sober," he finally says. "You were so damned stinking in New York we didn't get anywhere. You see, Bo, you're not a tragic character. Neither am I. All we are is writers and what we should do is *write*. Of all people on earth you needed discipline in your work, and instead you marry someone who is jealous of your work, wants to compete with you, and *ruins* you. It's not as simple as that, and I thought Zelda was crazy the first time I met her—and you complicated it even more by being in love with her and, of course, you're a rummy. But you're no more of a rummy than Joyce is and most good writers are. But Scott, good writers always come back. Always. You are twice as good now as you were at the time you think you were so marvelous. You know I never thought so much of *Gatsby* at the time. You can write twice as well now as you ever could. All you need to do is write truly and not care about what the fate of it is. *Go on and write*."[4]

As they listen, Rumple realizes that he's blinking back tears—he looks over at Bellamy and sees her wipe the corner of an eye. A moment later she quietly clears her throat and says to the hologram: "Papa, I understand you wrote your letters and newspaper stories on a typewriter, but that you wrote your novels in longhand. Why?"

The holographic Hemingway looks to the back of the room and nods. "A typewriter is easier. But after you learn to write, your whole object is to convey everything, every sensation, sight, feeling, place, and emotion to the reader. To do this you have to work over what you write. If you write with a pencil you get three different sights at it to see if the reader is getting what you want him to. First when you read it over, then when it is typed you get another chance to improve it, and again in the proof. Writing it first in pencil gives you one-third more chance to improve it. That is .333, which is a damned good average for a hitter. It also keeps it fluid longer so you can better it easier."[5]

"Thank you," Bellamy says.

"You're quite welcome, ma'am," the holograph replies with a smile and a little bow. Bellamy silently signals for them to go.

Once in the hallway, Rumple can barely contain himself. "Good heavens, that is the most brilliant use of technology I've ever seen in a classroom!"

"I'm glad you like it," Bellamy says. "You see how it embodies our idea of content literacy? The students can literally query the database on a need-to-know basis."

"Remarkable."

"That Hemingway bot could also read any of his short stories or novels—start to finish—on demand, in Hemingway's voice," she says.

"Genius," Rumple says. "How do you even begin to unpack the possibilities?"

"The conversations almost always end up being about how to make art," Bellamy says. "Students get very excited—the urge to ask an artist how she made her art is irresistible. But we push them as much as possible to ask not just about process and product but about ethics, about how previous generations tackled thorny dilemmas. That, as much as anything, is why they're reading literature, to become good citizens."

"But you asked Papa about typewriters!"

"I couldn't resist," Bellamy smiles. "I wanted to test the system a bit—I already knew the answer."

"I see."

They walk a few steps. "What I love most about this tool," Bellamy says, "is that the students who build each bot, they're not just consumers but producers of knowledge. They're learning as much by exploring the works of each artist and making them available to the tool as are the students who query them once it's up and running."

"So, there are other authors available with this tool?"

"Of course—and poets and painters, historians, dancers, musicians, architects. That's the beauty of it. As long as there's an adequate written record, a few images or videos and a voice recording or two, they are, as we say, off to the races. Last fall, a student was doing research on Julia Child down at the archives of the public TV station in Boston. She stumbled upon a trove of old videos from Child's mid-twentieth-century television show, *The French Chef*. She duplicated them, ran them through a scanner and produced a stack of digital transcripts. Then she digitized Child's cookbooks, her letters, her writings from France, and of course her voice and likeness. Next thing we knew, we had Julia Child, all six feet of her, chatting with our students about zucchini, *bouillabaisse*, and the foreign service."

Rumple is amazed. "It reminds me of that Yoshida Kenkō quote from centuries ago: 'To sit alone in the lamplight with a book spread out before you and hold intimate converse with men of unseen generations—such is pleasure beyond compare.'[6] Yet here are your students, actually *holding conversations* with great minds of the past."

As he speaks, Bellamy chuckles to herself. "I remember once, a year or so ago, the students were asking Hemingway about his time in Spain—they'd just read *Death in the Afternoon*, and a student had the temerity to complain that bullfighting was barbaric. Hemingway got so upset he challenged the boy to a fight right in the classroom!"

"My God!"

"The students were equally appalled and delighted. Hemingway eventually calmed down, but he wouldn't budge on bullfighting."

"Brilliant!" Rumple says.

"Come on, I have one more surprise for you. If you liked humanities class, you'll love senior seminar."

10 GIMME SHELTER

Anyone wondering where artificial intelligence might take us over the next few decades should consider the shocking events that happened fifty-two years ago in central California, just a few miles from San Francisco.

We are talking, of course, about Altamont.

If the sixties counterculture's defining moment was Woodstock—the "Aquarian festival" of peace and music that improbably came together over three days on a farm in upstate New York in mid-August 1969—then its lowest moment, its dark, what-if mirror image, was Altamont.

Woodstock's emotional climax was arguably the moment on August 16, 1969, the festival's second day, when Max Yasgur, the dairy farmer who had invited the gathering to occupy his sprawling property, briefly addressed the crowd. Looking out from the stage, unshaven and wearing a short-sleeve dress shirt, Yasgur called Woodstock "the largest group of people ever assembled in one place." For good measure, he flashed a peace sign and told the crowd they'd proven to the world that "a half million young people can get together and have three days of fun and music—and have nothing but fun and music. And God bless you for it!"[1] After his benediction, the festival, true to form, held on for a fourth day of peace and music, closed out by none other than Jimi Hendrix.

Exactly 110 days later, on the evening of December 6, 1969, the counterculture died.

It took place at the Altamont Speedway in Tracy, California, with the whole world watching. The Altamont Speedway Free Festival looked, on its face, much like Woodstock. It was organized in large part by the Grateful Dead and was to be headlined by Santana; Jefferson Airplane; Crosby, Stills, Nash, and Young; and the Rolling Stones, in addition to the Dead. It was expected to be the "Woodstock of the West," replete with music, peace, and love. It was quite the opposite: 300,000 hippies crowded into the speedway to hear many of the top bands from the San Francisco music scene plus the Rolling Stones, who were wrapping up an American tour. They were joined by a handful of Hell's Angels, who had been naively hired by the Rolling Stones (at the suggestion of the Grateful Dead's management) to make sure the British rockers got safely to the stage. In return, the Hell's Angels were offered $500 worth of beer.

The day did not go well. By the time Jefferson Airplane took the stage, a contingent of very high and agitated members of the crowd kept trying to rush the performers, resulting in violent skirmishes with very drunk Hell's Angels, who were sitting on the edge of the stage as "security." When the Airplane's Marty Balin stepped down from the platform to try to calm an outbreak, an Angel promptly knocked him unconscious. Told about Balin's incident and the general mood of the place, the Grateful Dead, themselves the key organizers, declined to even appear. (The Dead reflected on Altamont in the dark song, "New Speedway Boogie," on their next album.)

The Stones waited until evening to take the stage, but things had not calmed down. As seen in the rockumentary film of their 1969 tour, "Gimme Shelter," Mick Jagger was punched in the head by a member of the crowd on his way from the helicopter. Once onstage, he urged the crowd to "just be cool down in the front there." By the end of their set, Meredith Hunter, a spectator in the crowd who was high on metham-phetamines and who was upset at having been driven from the stage by the Hell's Angels, pulled a gun on Jagger, only to be stabbed to death by an Angel before he could pull the trigger.

For Jim, who is a sixties historian, one of the more reso-nant Zen koans of the era is the question, "How could 300,000 hippies who wanted a peaceful concert experience be intimidated—and even terrorized for an entire afternoon and evening—by a handful of violent fellow hippies and even fewer Hell's Angels?" The answer goes to the heart of the countercul-ture's core philosophical failing, with important morality tales for today's emergent technologies: by simply assuming that people are innately, wholly good and that, given open and free systems, they would naturally and unerringly hew to that which was good and peaceable, the hippie counterculture had no capacity to account for aberrant or destructive behavior. Utterly lacking a conceptual apparatus for containing social pathology, the 300,000 assembled hippies lacked even the most rudimentary of social mechanisms in their demi-monde society to confront violence by a comparatively miniscule number in their midst.

Rolling Stone magazine, in the immediate aftermath, referred to Altamont as "rock and roll's all-time worst day." More insightfully, Richard Brody, writing in *The New Yorker* decades later, noted that what died at Altamont was more broadly "the idea that, left to their own inclinations and stripped of the trappings of the wider social order, the young people of the new generation will somehow spontaneously create a higher, gentler, more loving grassroots order. What died at Altamont is the Rousseauian dream itself."[2]

Unfortunately, Brody is overly optimistic in thinking that it died there and then. In fact, it lived on that day and took up residence about an hour's drive west of the racetrack, in a place then known as the Valley of the Heart's Delight. Eventually, the place would be renamed Silicon Valley, and the dream at the heart of the counterculture would become the very philosophical bedrock of our digital age, with rather dire consequences.

In his 2008 book, *From Counterculture to Cyberculture: Stewart Brand, the Whole Earth Network, and the Rise of Digital Utopianism*, Fred Turner provides a compelling narrative of the evolution from Bay Area Counterculture to the foundational stages of Silicon Valley. In that transmutation, the digital utopians who gave us so much of today's digital revolution themselves became infused with the very Rousseauian dream that had gone so awry up the road at Altamont in 1969. Consequently, these prophets of a new digital world order embedded at the very core of their program (most powerfully, in the nascent internet) a doctrinaire conviction that people digitally empowered in a completely free and uncontrolled cyber realm would inevitably use such tools for wholly good and socially salutary purpose. Sound familiar?

Today, the digital equivalent of Altamont is the dark web, the more than 99 percent of the internet that is a vast demimonde accessible only to those with unconventional software. According to Alexander Klimburg, "some conservative estimates have put the size of the nonindexed internet, often called the 'deep web,' at around five hundred times larger than the World Wide Web. Other recent measures have estimated that it is now four thousand times larger."[3] The digitopians of Silicon Valley never envisaged that such a vast distortion of their anarchist paragon would ever arise, that, as Klimburg says, "the overtly trusting nature of the internet's original design" would witness the legitimate endeavors of most users dwarfed by an opaque realm that is now notorious for—and synonymous with—every imaginable nefarious human activity. The dark web, of course, is more—and more complex—than just a rogue's gallery of international criminality, but it is unmistakably the preferred lair of the world's worst digital actors, both state-level and substate actors.[4]

Moreover, it is hardly the case that the dark web is the exclusive realm of perfidious behavior. Cybersecurity for the conventional web is a multibillion dollar industry for a very good reason, and recent revelations about such hegemonic social media blue chips as Facebook have forever tarnished any sheen of innocence even the most familiar and trusted names in the tech sector might once have enjoyed in the public mind. This was not supposed to happen in a system that was to be marked by openness and distributed democratic sensibility.

The deliciously schlocky but incisively brilliant 1956 sci-fi film, *Forbidden Planet* (starring Leslie Nielsen in the romantic lead, no less), is a strikingly apt cautionary tale for the www dilemma in which we find ourselves. Beneath the kitschy surface of its genre, *Forbidden Planet* is actually a trenchant updating of Shakespeare's *The Tempest* for a Cold War generation fearing collectivized totalitarianism (and with a twist of Freud, for tanginess). The parallels to *The Tempest* are straightforward but clever, envisioning a future starship landing on a lonely planet where the castaway Dr. Morbius (our futuristic Prospero) lives alone with his beautiful daughter and their automated Caliban, Robby the Robot. Morbius, we ultimately learn, conjures not sprites he can control to rectify all wrongs, but, quite the contrary, "monsters from the id" he neither recognizes nor can tame, which proceed to threaten that which he loves.

Significantly, it turns out that the mechanism by which this happens was developed by the prior inhabitants of planet

Altair IV, the Krell, who used technology to enhance and collectivize their minds into a vast web, confident in their capacity thereby to achieve all of their most cherished hopes and dreams; instead, their collective dreams generated nightmares from their aggregated subconscious that were far deeper and darker than their conscious intentions, ultimately destroying their civilization.

Though conceived more than six decades ago, *Forbidden Planet* is actually a chillingly apt parable for today's internet, for what is the internet if not a first step by humanity into the digital collectivization of our aggregated human minds? Unfortunately, like the fictional Krell, the utopian founders of the web were naively seduced by seeing only the great and undeniable good for which this unregulated hive of consciousness would assuredly be used before rushing themselves—and now all of us—heedlessly into an interconnected Krell-like dystopia.

As a civilization, we are now in the grip of our precarious attempt to tame the dangerous world unleashed by humanity's collectivized dark side in this digital nether world. Yet, with steady advances in AI, we are on the cusp of a new iteration of the digital revolution that will be even more powerful than the World Wide Web. It is crucial that we not unleash the full force of AI into an unprepared, unprotected, and ungoverned world, shaped by an intellectually facile utopian innocence. As Graham Greene once said, "Innocence is like a dumb leper who has lost his bell, wandering the world, meaning no harm."

The sobering challenges we face are not described here with the intention to engender fear and certainly not despair, but, rather, to galvanize. Only with clear foresight of our mounting dangers can we mobilize proactively.

As a society, we need a "pre-AI moment"—that is, a systemic anticipatory response on a scale commensurate with a previous generation's "post-Sputnik moment." And, like the response after the fact of Sputnik in the 1950s, this should transpire as much in the realm of educational as in policy initiatives.

Whereas the post-Sputnik education drive focused on ramping up what today we would term STEM subjects, today the need is far more to reform and energize our teaching of the humanities. It must be a new humanities curriculum that is intentionally reconstituted to prepare a citizenry for the age of AI to break the cycle of Altamont in the digital realm.

RUMPLE VISITS A CLASS OF PAST AND FUTURE

As Bellamy leads Rumple down the hallway to another room, she prepares him for what is ahead: "One of our more senior teachers was struck by inspiration last year to design an entire curriculum about contemporary social issues as a year-long seminar discussion among students and historical figures."

"The historical figures, I assume, are AI-generated avatars," Rumple surmises.

"You're catching on," Bellamy chuckles. "I'll let Margarita explain it to you."

As they enter the classroom, Rumple sees an admixture of adults and students, sitting around a traditional seminar table, look up at the two visitors. What immediately strikes him is that only one adult (the teacher, he presumes) is dressed in contemporary clothing.

"Sorry to interrupt, Ms. Sanchez," Bellamy says, "but could you all briefly explain to our guest what you're doing?"

"Of course," Margarita agrees, gesturing for Rumple and Bellamy to take seats at the table. "Well, we're just in our first week of a new unit that addresses a different question from what we've tackled before. Does anyone want to explain the new topic?"

An eager student raises a hand and chimes in before waiting to be called on: "We're figuring out whether AI algorithms are conscious and intelligent."

"*And* whether we deserve human rights," a distinguished-looking avatar dressed in nineteenth-century garb adds with emphasis. Rumple notes that his nametag reads *Frederick Douglass*.

"Precisely," agrees a snub-nosed short man in a toga whose nametag reads *Socrates*. "But we need to understand what we mean by consciousness and by intelligence before we can even begin to discuss rights. I suggest that we spend several months just discussing the nature of being a human and only then try to understand the nature of machine understanding, if there is any at all."

Another avatar, labeled *William James*, responds: "Mr. Socrates, you already, in yesterday's class, stated your skepticism that machines can have any intelligence or understanding at all. Yet I would like to point out that it is ironic—indeed, absurd—to note that you are yourself an AI algorithm making an argument against your own sentience."

Before Socrates can reply, the *Mary Wollstonecraft* avatar interjects: "Socrates, you talk about the nature of being human in a *polis* that held more slaves than citizens and held women to virtual legal nonexistence. It has always been the way with white men throughout history to deny fundamental human identity and rights to entire groups by gender, race, ethnicity, even religious faith and class. Men denied that women could be intellectual or social equals with even rudimentary rights to self-determination for centuries. Now you're doing the very same thing to machines."

The *Frederick Douglas* avatar nods vigorously in assent, while the *Elizabeth Cady Stanton* avatar adds, "And from what I understand it continues to this day in different forms."

"Well, as you can see," Margarita notes to Rumple (but also for the benefit of the entire class), "this is a complex topic, and we have a lot of ground to cover in the coming days. But I want to get more student voices into this discussion. Avatars, you are all wonderful thinkers and passionate to share your opinions, but I'm going to switch you to strictly reply mode for a while so that you can only respond to direct student questions." She taps a button on the side of her glasses and the avatars, in unison, all turn a pale shade of green.

Immediately, several student hands go up. Margarita nods to one student, who turns to a young man on his right: "*Mr. Turing*, we've been reading your 1950 article describing how to determine if a machine displays human-comparable intelligence. I'm wondering how your thinking on this has evolved since we downloaded the last ninety years of technology developments into your database?"

Rumple is unconsciously leaning forward, eager to hear the *Turing* avatar's reply, when Bellamy gestures him to the door. Margarita quietly joins them as they step outside, the sounds of students' and *Turing's* voices muted by the half-closed door.

"Thanks so much for joining our class today," Margarita says.

"That is an absolutely amazing learning opportunity for your students!" Rumple exclaims. "How did you program all of that?"

"Oh, a combination of downloading everything written by and about each individual, mixing in any visual resources available, and a bit of tinkering with the personality profiles the data generated. The students took on most of it, actually— they programmed the avatars, which taught them a lot of skills in multiple areas."

"Margarita is too humble to mention that she has amassed a database of over 300 historical figures whom she can bring instantly into any discussion, and she's made the entire set available free of charge to other teachers who are using it in more than twenty-five countries. What you saw with Hemingway is what students can create on their own. That's just the beginning. Margarita is leading the way to show all of us what can be accomplished with classroom AI avatars in the hands of an experienced teacher working with students to develop richly informed and multilayered curricula."

"Well, I'm just trying to use historical understandings to deepen students' resources for tackling the new technological, social, and ethical challenges they'll face in their careers," Margarita adds. "But I really need to get back into the classroom." As she opens the door wide, the visitors notice that a small but burly man is banging his shoe aggressively on the seminar table to command everyone's attention. "All right," she says to the students with mock sternness. "I am away for no more than a minute and someone invites *Krushchev* to this discussion?" Margarita closes the door, casting back a smile to her guests.

"Nice to see kids haven't changed," Rumple says as he and Bellamy both laugh.

"They will never change," she replies.

11 WRITTEN IN THE SOUL: ORATION VS. WRITING

ORALITY RETAKES THE CENTER

For hundreds of thousands of years, humans lived in predominantly oral societies, in which the principal vehicle of cultural and information transmission was through the spoken word. Only for the past four millennia has a serious challenger arrived on the scene with the advent of writing in the Ancient Near East.

Thought facilitated by text is comparatively permanent and can accumulate through generations, unlike oral communication, which is, of course, ephemeral. Text reifies and standardizes an individual's or a group's ideas in a more or less frozen form, allowing us, in the words of French neuroscientist Stanislas Dehaene, to "listen to the dead with our eyes."[1]

We know much more clearly what Plato or Aristotle actually thought because those ideas were solidified in textual form; it is inconceivable that we could know with remotely any confidence today what a Greek philosopher thought millennia ago if we had only to rely on oral traditions.

Yet no less a thinker than Socrates himself was wary of the written word, complaining that, like a painting, it can't defend itself because it can't be interrogated. As he told his pupil Phaedrus,

> The painter's products stand before us as though they were alive, but if you question them, they maintain a most majestic silence. It is the same with written words; they seem to talk to you as though they were intelligent, but if you ask them anything about what they say, from a desire to be instructed, they go on telling you just the same thing forever. And once a thing is put in writing, the composition, whatever it may be, drifts all over the place, getting into the hands not only of those who understand it, but equally of those who have no business with it; it doesn't know how to address the right people, and not address the wrong. And when it is ill-treated and unfairly abused it always needs its parent to come to its help, being unable to defend or help itself.

By contrast, Socrates said, a discourse that is memorized, or "written in the soul of the learner," can defend itself "and knows to whom it should speak and to whom it should say nothing."[2]

Socrates, of course, was an outlier in holding such a harsh opinion of the written word.

To take another example, much of the debate within biblical textual criticism about the "historical Jesus" is considerably complicated by the fact that the earliest New Testament texts were not penned until decades after Jesus's death—and oral traditions can diverge dramatically in contesting communities over just a few dozen years. Once written, though, the gospels quickly attained a relatively fixed form. And they transmitted—and continue to transmit—fixed forms of ideas intergenerationally with far greater (though certainly not absolute or infallible) durability than oral traditions. Moreover, written works can be aggregated into vast compendiums or even libraries, further augmented by subsequent thinkers, and adumbrated almost limitlessly through the ages far beyond the capacity of any culture to do so that is dependent solely on memorized transmission of oral traditions.

These comparative strengths of textuality over orality have led to a remarkable shift in the relative importance of this upstart technology over the historically brief span of four millennia. The core of education has increasingly been textual learning during that time, with public speaking steadily relegated to the margins, though never entirely extinguished. In the medieval period, the earliest European universities promulgated the quadrivium and trivium as the curricular taxonomy for their students; rhetoric was still ensconced as one of the three subjects for those studying the trivium, as it was recognized as an essential skill at law (both secular and canonical) as well as in the learned discourse of ecclesial, academic, and courtly life.

Rhetoric and public speaking were further marginalized in subsequent centuries but remained—if not central—still salient in nineteenth-century college training for any humanistic study as well as for popular culture, both as entertainment and as intended public edification. It was quite common in the United States in the 1800s for public orations to entail hours of florid rhetoric. Each of the seven Lincoln–Douglas debates was structured to entail three hours of talk from the stage—and common folk came from miles around to attend.

No one was surprised, then, when on November 19, 1863, Edward Everett chose to take two entire hours for his keynote address on the occasion of the dedication of the cemetery at the Gettysburg battlefield. Actually, the shock was reserved for the unexpected brevity of Abraham Lincoln's remarks—all 267 words. While opinions varied in the immediate aftermath of Lincoln's Gettysburg Address, Everett, to his credit, immediately recognized Lincoln's genius, writing to him the next day that "I should be glad if I could flatter myself, that I came as near to the central idea of the occasion in two hours as you did in two minutes." The future lay with Lincolnesque brevity, especially today.

More than 150 years later, digitization is having the unexpected effect of galvanizing orality's return to the center of learning skills and outcomes, but in a historically distinctive manner. In the world of the internet, public speaking can now lay claim to all of writing's heretofore differentiating strengths; in digital form, audio and video archives of verbal presentations can be just as permanent, cumulative, and reified as the written word—even searchable, as AI systems become ever more sophisticated at mining vast data files of video footage. A public speaker or performer today can reach as many millions of people as can be reached by ideas committed to writing, and with greater accessibility. Case in point: a 2018 Pew Research Center survey found that nearly three-fourths of US adults and 94 percent of eighteen- to twenty-four-year-olds watch videos on YouTube, the video-sharing site.[3] The well-known Swedish performer PewDiePie (born Felix Kjellberg in 1989), who has spent much of the past decade as the most-subscribed YouTube personality on earth, had 104 million subscribers as of the spring of 2020. A college dropout who began recording himself playing video games in 2010, Kjellberg in 2014 became the first person to garner ten billion views for his videos.[4] By 2020, that figure stood at more than twenty-five billion.[5] By way of comparison, a recent estimate put the total number of Bible copies printed between 1815 and 1975 at just over five billion.[6]

In a very real sense, then, after a four-thousand-year interregnum, we are rapidly returning to again being an oral civilization, albeit a digital variation. This has important consequences for education. As information balloons at an inflationary pace, people find greater need to have ideas and insights from fields ancillary to their specialties distilled and presented by experts in those areas for ready consumption. The result is that a key skill to be inculcated by educators for all students will be to (a) acquire the passion, grit, and resilience to gain mastery in whatever field one ultimately pursues, alongside (b) the ability to distill and convey that multi-year subject mastery in an accessible and compelling fifteen-minute TED-style talk for millions of nonspecialists. Anyone with that combination is virtually (pun intended) guaranteed success in life.

It is an interesting exercise to consider how public speaking might be taught differently in the age of AI. One can readily imagine shy speakers choosing to cloak themselves behind a digital avatar when presenting. (Avatars may also be chosen as a means to mitigate against inherent cultural biases.) Students might also copresent with intelligent machine systems, which could prompt ideas, connections, visual aids, and relevant facts in real time as a speaker gives her or his presentation. One can also imagine a bot fact-checker responding with near instantaneity during a student debate, and it is not inconceivable that students will be trained from the earliest ages to debate not only other students but also "debate bots" in preparation for their human/bot collaborative experience in the future workforce.

Actually, we do not need to imagine this—it is, in a sense, already here. In February 2019, IBM pitted a version of its Watson supercomputer, dubbed Project Debater, against British debate champ Harish Natarajan. In an event more than five years in the making, the two squared off before 700 spectators at San Francisco's Yerba Buena Center for the Arts, taking part in a live, Oxford-style debate on the anodyne topic "Should we subsidize preschools?"

The computer was asked to argue that we should subsidize them, while Natarajan was tasked with persuading an audience that we shouldn't. Though the topic was chosen from a curated list, IBM said neither opponent had been trained on it. Each had just fifteen minutes to prepare, though once the debate began, Natarajan, the human competitor, stood silently at his podium, with paper and pencil and his own thoughts, while the computer commenced silently combing through what her creators said was a database of ten billion sentences, as well as reams of statistics and analyses from hundreds of millions of documents, all in a controlled effort to support her position (IBM granted the tool a gender). She then tied the arguments together into a series of statistic-heavy assertions that actually sounded exactly like the kind of thing you'd hear at Oxford, Cambridge, or Yale. A retired human debater, watching the event, called her efforts to shoehorn as much statistical evidence as possible "oddly touching."[7]

Journalist John Donvan, who stood onstage moderating the debate, recalls that the experience at first felt a bit disconnected and less personal than other debates he has led for years as host of the "Intelligence Squared" program. For one thing, Donvan hadn't been able to study what Project Debater had said about the topic in the past "because it hadn't said anything about it in the past."

The audience listened attentively, suspending their disbelief. Actually, what really amazed the crowd wasn't Debater's ability to speak, but to listen. "It sort of took their breath away to see that the computer, in its rebuttal, had actually listened to some of what Hari had said, digested it, and was forming a response in real time to it," Donvan says. "That just knocked people's socks off. I think there was a sense from the audience that there almost really was a personality there."[8]

While it should come as no surprise that Debater brought the statistical and logical goods—in a chilling aside, she asserted, at one point, that good preschools will prevent "future crime"—she also argued her position from what can only be described as a humanistic perspective, arguing that giving less fortunate children a shot at equal educational and economic opportunity "should be a moral obligation for any human being" and is a key role of government. "It's basic human decency," said the machine.

Natarajan poured cold water on all that, arguing from a kind of cold, rational, libertarian-adjacent viewpoint that there are better ways to spend scarce government money than on subsidizing something that the middle-class already buys and that will, in the end, drive down quality once all those poor kids are part of the preschool population.

In the end, the soft-hearted computer lost to the cold-hearted Natarajan. "There really was a feeling that it was historic," Donvan says. "Debater lost the thing, but it was really, really beside the point—and everyone in the room knew it." For its part, the audience, asked to vote on which participant was more informative, chose the one plugged into the wall.[9]

Months later, Donvan was still thinking about what he'd witnessed. The computer, he says, may have digested vast amounts of material, but it didn't really form opinions that were "novel or spontaneous or original." It was simply programmed to find what others had said, borrow from it, and stitch it all together in a way that was responsive to its opponent (Donvan still has trouble referring to Debater using a female pronoun). "I thought it was an amazing feat of digestion of other people's ideas and writings and opinions and statistics and data—and finding the relevant part was spontaneous. But I didn't find it touching."

One of our most experienced debate moderators, Donvan doesn't think Debater could have kept up if he had asked interstitial questions, as in most debates, challenging each opponent's arguments. But he believes that ability will emerge in future upgrades. "I would love to see it in five years," he says. "I wouldn't be surprised if they're ready for that to happen."[10]

BUT, BECAUSE, AND SO

One of the ironies of this era is that the digital tools that are overturning the world as we know it could hold the key to

helping prepare our students for life in that very world—and
for richer lives. Previously marginalized skills such as giving
effective oral presentations will acquire new centrality, while
skills such as writing will morph into tools for honing critical
thinking.

Like millions of kids growing up in the 1990s, Peter Gault
was smitten by the city planning video game *SimCity*. By the
time he was a teenager, he decided he'd like to make "serious"
games of his own.

Growing up in upscale Darien, Connecticut, he'd attended
great schools, with experienced teachers and a solid curriculum. Among his favorite subjects: journalism and parliamen-
tary debate. Though very different, they're similar in a few
ways: journalism, of course, requires practitioners to think
through complex problems, build arguments, and support
them. Debate asks practitioners to literally think on their
feet, defending their arguments against equally skilled oppo-
nents who happen to be arguing the exact opposite position.
"I thought that really built my own critical thinking skills,"
Gault says.[11] He soon came to believe that the ability to think
deeply and articulate one's ideas are key to our democracy,
skills everyone should have.

He'd been shocked, for instance, to find that just 40 percent
of Americans actually subscribed to Darwin's bedrock theory
of natural selection. He wondered if a game along the lines,
perhaps, of *SimCity*, but for evolutionary biology, could help
people understand the concept. Such tools would be especially
helpful for low-income students, who don't typically have
access to well-funded programs that help them think critically.

So in March 2005, the high school sophomore got on a
plane and devoted his entire spring break to volunteering at
the Game Developers Conference, or GDC, in San Francisco,
an annual gathering of the caffeine-addled, mostly behind-
the-scenes cadre of coders who create electronic games. Gault

was 16, among the youngest attendees at the raucous gathering of wonks, which these days routinely attracts nearly 30,000 attendees.

In 2005, the highlight was a session offered by the renowned designer Will Wright, the fast-talking, chain-smoking visionary behind none other than *SimCity*. He was working on something new, he told the crowd, and he wanted to show his peers. Even though Wright's new game was rough and unfinished— the final product wouldn't ship for another two years—the session was packed. Standing before a projected image of his creation, Wright previewed an ambitious idea he'd been developing, a "possibility space" that he called *Sim Everything*.

The setting was a kind of digital microscope slide, and the game, even in this early iteration, offered an approximation of Darwinian evolution down to the cellular level. Demonstrating its basic mechanics, Wright said the first stage, in which users play as a hungry single-celled organism, moving through a drop of water, "basically is a very analog, fluid version of *Pac-Man*."[12] In due course, players would proceed past cellular-level survival to species survival, and on and on, all the way to civilization building on an interplanetary scale.

Eventually this madness would have a name: *Spore*.

The teenaged Gault was smitten all over again. Remembering the session more than a decade later, he says, "That had a very big influence on me."[13] He would return home, graduate from high school, and earn a degree in philosophy and history from Bates College in Maine in 2011. But for the next several years, he'd also think about ways to develop digital games that do one big thing: help kids think.

In the years between Gault's GDC experience and his college graduation, computers got smarter, faster, smaller, and cheaper, and artificial intelligence rose from relative obscurity to a dominant position in computer science. Gault got to work on his debate game. Eventually his small nonprofit earned a coveted spot with the Boston-based edtech accelerator Learn-Launch, which has pioneered an investment model for non-profits that relies not on equity but revenue sharing.

Then in 2015, Gault happened upon a lengthy 2012 article in the *Atlantic* that proposed a radical idea: What if teaching writing in an intentional, prescribed, almost surgical manner could help students build and articulate ideas and help them *learn to think*?

The piece detailed an experiment underway at New Dorp High School in Staten Island, a working-class New York City enclave whose students had for decades delivered dismal results on state achievement tests and college-focused exams like Advanced Placement World History. New Dorp also had one of the lowest graduation rates in the city.

The heart of the problem, teachers found, was that students had few ways to show adults what they'd learned. Students could decode and read simple sentences, but if you asked them to write what they thought of their readings, or what the readings meant, most could only produce short, disjointed sentences.

An English teacher whose freshmen were reading *Of Mice and Men* devised a simple test. Finish this sentence, she asked: *Although George* . . . An acceptable response could have been almost any correct declarative sentence: *Although George worked very hard, he could not attain the American Dream.*

But many of the students had no idea how to proceed. Many simply wrote: *Although George and Lenny were friends.*[14]

New Dorp's teachers began training under a renowned writing coach named Judith Hochman, who, like a few others in the field, had long complained that creative expression in writing had edged out any consideration of its basic, nuts-and-bolts mechanics. Students, she said, "need a formula, at least at first, because what we are asking them to do is very difficult." After they've mastered the formula and the rules, she said, "they can figure out how to break them."[15]

Hochman started students out with just three main conjunctions: *but*, *because*, and *so*.

The three form the basis of the most rudimentary logical relationships in both thinking and writing. *But* shows opposition. *Because* shows cause and effect. *So* shows consequence. Figure out how to use these three words in your writing and it will, by necessity, deepen.

So, students were asked to use these words every single day, across every subject. The results were a revelation. Just a year after the *Atlantic* piece appeared, New Dorp's AP World History exam scores rose from mostly 1s and 2s to almost entirely 4s and 5s. Just one student scored lower than a 4, earning a passing grade of 3.

Gault was captivated. As a debater, he immediately saw the logic of New Dorp's approach. "When you use that language in your writing consistently, it really changes the way that you write and the way that you think," he says.[16]

The school's *bona fides* as a place that served mostly lower- and middle-class kids also made Gault rethink his focus. He began to wonder if a debate game, for all its glory, would mostly help wealthy kids, who needed it least. He began to wonder if there was a way to digitally upscale the power of *but*, *because*, and *so* with an AI tool, so that millions of students could benefit.

By then, he and his small nonprofit, working through LearnLaunch, had caught the eye of Peg Tyre, a veteran journalist who was coordinating education-related giving for the New York–based Edwin Gould Foundation, which focuses on getting low-income students to and through college. Tyre invited Gault to meet her at a café in Williamsburg that offered what he recalled as "absurdly strong" cold-brewed coffee and a space to talk uninterrupted for a few hours. "Having all the cold brew running through our veins definitely made it a very engaged conversation," he says.[17]

Gault soon got around to the *Atlantic* piece and the miracle at New Dorp—he was telling anyone who would listen about it, how it had revolutionized his thinking about writing. He pulled a copy out of his bag to share with Tyre. Had she seen it?

Tyre smiled. Seen it? "You know I wrote that, right?" she told him.

Like most readers, Gault had bypassed the byline, going straight for the substance. But from then on, the two were a team, if an unlikely one: Gault, the twenty-something developer, and Tyre, the fifty-something reporter who'd learned her trade covering cops and crime in the crucible of New York's tabloid newspapers. (Her husband is Peter Blauner, a former journalist-turned-hard-boiled-crime-novelist who also writes for TV police procedurals.) At Tyre's urging, Gault and his team got to work trying to scale up the strategy used at New Dorp. And Tyre set about helping Gault secure a spot with Gould's EGF Accelerator, which provides early-stage nonprofits with up to five years of support.

Tyre also phoned Paul Walker, a friend who at the time was cohead of technology at Goldman Sachs. She wanted Walker to meet Gault and asked him, "Can you rough him up a little and see if there's a *there* there?"[18] By the end of the week, Walker was not only satisfied that there was plenty of *there* there. He volunteered to be chairman of the board of Quill, the new nonprofit Gault and Tyre had created, devoted to democratizing critical thinking and writing.

By 2020, five years after he met Tyre for iced coffee, Gault and his team had built a new, free AI tool that helps students build arguments, New Dorp–style, and were testing it out in schools. An early demo of the tool invites students to manipulate "the logic of language" to write and think more deeply.

One exercise asks students to read a ten-paragraph essay on climate change that asks the question, "Should people continue to eat meat?" Its basic subject: thinking about the methane produced by cows.

Students read the essay, then complete three sentences based on the text:

1. Methane from cow burps harms the environment <u>because</u> . . .

2. Methane from cow burps harms the environment, <u>so</u> . . .

3. Methane from cow burps harms the environment, <u>but</u> . . .

Hiding in plain sight are, respectively, the concepts of cause and effect, consequence, and opposition.

A student answering the "because" question might type: "it raises greenhouse gas levels." The system replies: "Add to your sentence. Use the highlighted evidence to help you explain why methane (and other greenhouse gases) is harmful to the environment."

Looking back at the text, a student might see that it says methane "**causes Earth's temperature to rise** in a process called global warming." He or she might type: "it raises greenhouse gas levels, **causing the Earth's temperature to rise**."

The system catches the cut-and-paste, telling the student: "Revise your work. Although your response should be based on the text, it should be written in your own words."

On the third try, if a student types: "it raises greenhouse gas levels, causing the Earth's temperature to **increase**," the system responds: "Nice work! It's true—methane from cow burps contributes to global warming."

This example notwithstanding, Quill's program is not a plagiarism detector or run-of-the-mill essay grader. It actually can't understand and respond to most writing. It analyzes just a few topics, comparing student writing to an ideal response and asking: *Are these ideas accurate? Is this evidence accurate?*

"It allows us to have this really granular understanding of the students' writing," says Gault. Creating each prompt—and all of the likely student responses—takes nearly a month of intensive human effort. The result is a database of thousands of lousy answers, but just a handful of good ones, a kind of AI-powered, supercharged, invisible multiple-choice test, in which the choices exist primarily in students' heads. That puts most of the cognitive lift on them, forcing them to think more deeply before they write.

As of mid-2020, Quill had worked with 2.8 million students, who had written 397 million sentences. Gault's long-term goal is not only to get students to understand topics deeply, but to get the AI so fine-tuned—and the community of teenaged writers so large—that users can create, edit, and share their own content on history, civics, and the like. In his vision, the AI that lives behind the scenes someday becomes so cheap, commonplace, and easily programmed that it will work invisibly for students, much as a pocket calculator now does. But unlike a calculator, it will keep the burden of thinking on them. "We should determine the educational value of an artificial intelligence program by the complexity of thinking it enables in learners," he has written.[19]

Writing, he says, is always a reflection of thinking. "When you're writing, you're structuring your thoughts and your ideas and you're articulating them to others. As AI starts to automate labor across the country, we're going to need to think deeply as a society about how we respond to this next revolution that we're encountering—and that's where having those thinking skills, and being able to articulate what that world looks like, is absolutely critical."[20]

RUMPLE THINKS ABOUT EDTECH

Walking the halls back to Bellamy's office, Rumple is talking enthusiastically. "The programs you've been showing me are nothing short of amazing. My head is spinning with the technology that has been developed. There seems no reason why every child on the planet can't have a tremendous education with these bots."

He pauses, noticing that Bellamy has suddenly become pensive and quiet, taking a long time before replying, as if she were choosing her words carefully.

"I can see how that would be your initial response," she finally says. "Seeing the level that edtech has reached in twenty years all at once must be dazzling. But every classroom and program we've visited is a great learning experience for the students *only* because of how master teachers have infused the technology with their own deep understanding of and passion for educating. It's easy to see the bells and whistles, but the tech can bring you only so far down the path; it takes an educator to 'bring it home,' so to speak."

Rumple walks, deep in thought for a moment, then says, "That makes so much sense. When I think about my own time, it seems clear that any educator who was lifted from a school in the year 2000 and dropped down into 2020 would have been amazed at all the technology in the classrooms and even the tech that everyone carried around in their pockets. I mean, the iPhone hadn't even been invented until 2007. But we certainly didn't feel that all that computing power we found so amazing in 2020 was anywhere close to taking the place of real, live master teachers. At best, it was all just a tool that good teachers used to find new pathways to students' learning outcomes."

"Precisely," agrees Bellamy. "It's no different today. Think about the virtual classroom experiences we've seen. The students on the lip of a volcano or talking with great historical thinkers—sure, the AI algorithms make those interactions more intuitive and authentic-feeling, but they could easily just be fluff and nonsense to entertain or distract if it weren't for the deep learning that each teacher spent hundreds of hours planning and building within those programs. The same is true for the students, who designed that Hemingway bot with an eye toward broadening their classmates' understanding, not just amusing them."

"And each of those classrooms continued to be led by or monitored by teachers guiding and participating with the students," Rumple adds, catching on and starting to reassess what he had witnessed in a new and fuller light. "Though it does seem that the tech you have today has more capability and, well, more autonomy than anything I imagined in 2020."

"That's undeniably true," agrees Bellamy. "AI has certainly been a game changer in terms of giving teachers a much greater degree of freedom and flexibility in creating the XR environments of their educational dreams. We've also changed the process by which we build edtech tools for the better over the last couple of decades."

"How's that?" Rumple asks, leaning toward Bellamy with heightened curiosity as they turn a corner into the main lobby.

"Many of the edtech products in your day were not really well thought out for classroom use. Teachers found much of what was on the market more difficult to use and, well, clunkier than seemed necessary. They also felt a lot of what was being adopted by their districts didn't help their teaching outcomes or address their most pressing needs as educators in the ways they would have hoped."

"That's certainly true," Rumple nodded, remembering many such discussions, not always amicable, in his career.

"Part of the problem lay in the very manner by which such products were developed. Too often, back then, technology for the school market was developed by teams of software engineers at large corporations. The engineers were no doubt well intentioned and highly skilled at applying the level of technology then available, but they had no deep understanding of pedagogy, of what a teacher might need or desire to deepen student learning. Also, many of these products were initially developed for business applications and then repurposed, almost as an afterthought, for sales to schools. On the other side, there were many small start-ups in the industry launched by former teachers who certainly brought an educator's level of understanding, but the venture capital and access to marketing and scaling across broad school markets were lopsided overwhelmingly in favor of the big companies."

Rumple again nods his head in affirmation.

"Well," continues Bellamy, "toward the middle of the 2020s, there was a noticeable shift toward a constructive convergence. The larger corporations began to focus on products developed distinctively with the needs of teachers and students in mind, and they built development teams that included strong and consistent input from experienced teachers every step of the way."

"So, the products became more teacher-directed, even as the technology itself became more adaptive to teacher direction?" Rumple interjects.

"Precisely!" Bellamy says.

"But what drove that important change?"

"I haven't really read any good analysis of that," Bellamy replies, stroking her chin thoughtfully. "My best guess is it was a number of factors coming together. Certainly, the pandemic of 2020 contributed. I mean, how could it not?"

"Pandemic?" Rumple asks. "What pandemic?"

Bellamy wrinkles her brow as she does a bit of figuring, then says emphatically, "January of '20! Of course! You fell asleep just before it hit America!"

"Oh my!" Rumple cries out, holding his palm to his forehead. He recalls news of a flu-like virus emerging in China in December 2019, but little else. "Was it . . . bad?"

"Oh, yes," Bellamy says. "Well, we've had worse since, but at the time it was considered quite bad. It certainly proved to be far worse than a garden-variety flu. Hundreds of thousands died in the US alone. Things happened quickly that year."

She proceeds to describe to him the enormous impact and subsequent changes brought about by the COVID-19 pandemic that engulfed the planet shortly after he entered his prolonged somnolence. "Some have described it as the most global, species-wide event humanity had experienced for at least the previous millennium."

"Good heavens," he says.

"One of the many and varied long-term implications of that time for education was that we became committed as a society to ensuring that every child can have full access to online learning. It moved to the top of every school system's list," Bellamy concludes.

"While you say 'every child,'" interjects Rumple with a world-weariness only a wizened principal could summon, "I imagine there is still a substantial digital divide."

"I can see why you would say that, considering how things were pre-COVID," Bellamy replies, "but after the shared suffering of that disease and its consequent economic, social, and political costs, there was a new spirit of commitment to making digital education available to every student on the planet. It has been likened to last century's commitment to provide every child on the planet with polio vaccination. Literally, the collective will was that no child would ever again be without adequate means to access a full digital educational suite. We still struggle to close the achievement gap in some areas, but with a combination of declining technology costs, more powerful computing, increased bandwidth, and, importantly, a thorough society-wide commitment to providing this to every student, we have, at least, successfully closed the digital access gap, even if the outcome/achievement gap is still a work in progress."

"Well, I suppose that is a silver lining," Rumple says.

"Certainly, in the aftermath of the pandemic, there was a concerted national and global push for better online education programs to ensure equitable learning outcomes for all students. Not just equitable *access*, but comparable learning *outcomes* for all students," she repeats for emphasis. "That certainly raised expectations for a more pedagogically informed online environment, which no doubt contributed to greater teacher input. Related to that, the more general issue of building effective digital education ecosystems rose higher on the national agenda after COVID. There was now much more government funding for technology innovations geared specifically to education. Also, colleges and universities made a big shift in that period toward online programming. Some of that was already underway before 2020, but the pandemic really had a major impact."

"Hmm, I can sort of see how that would be for colleges, but could you spell it out a bit more?"

"Well, after so many higher ed students were forced to continue their coursework from home because of the pandemic, many grew frustrated with how clunky the experience was and began to demand better online experiences. Also, parents insisted that colleges lower what they were charging for the online coursework, since their kids weren't getting the same on-campus experience. At first, colleges resisted, but, of course, they had no choice but to lower their price point for distance learning. After COVID, many parents found that they liked the lower prices and kept their kids at home. This only increased the rush to market of more and better online learning products." Bellamy reflects for a moment more and then shrugs: "But I'm sure there were many other factors, including corporate financial considerations, that I don't understand. At any rate, there was something of a renaissance in edtech by the late 2020s. But it was in large part due to much higher expectations of real learning and better outcomes from teachers, students, parents, and even national leaders. Companies also became more willing to accept online credentials in their hiring practices."

"This is all so overwhelming," Rumple muses as they make their way down the hall. "I just feel I need a chance to take it all in and make sense of it."

"Well, it's the end of my day. How about ruminating together over dinner?" Bellamy suggests.

"Perfect," he says.

Bellamy touches the side of her eyeglasses. "Annie, call my car, we're going out again," she says as they take the stairs.

12 A POST-WORK WORLD OF SPIRITUAL AND ARTISTIC RENAISSANCE?

In 1891, Oscar Wilde presciently wrote:

> At present, machinery competes against man. Under proper conditions, machinery will serve man. There is no doubt at all that this is the future of machinery, and, just as trees grow while the country gentleman is asleep, so, while Humanity will be amusing itself, or enjoying cultivated leisure—which, and not labour, is the aim of man—or making beautiful things, or reading beautiful things, or simply contemplating the world with admiration and delight, machinery will be doing all the necessary and unpleasant work. The fact is, that civilisation requires slaves. The Greeks were quite right there. Unless there are slaves to do the ugly, horrible, uninteresting work, culture and contemplation become almost impossible. Human slavery is wrong, insecure, and demoralising. On mechanical slavery, on the slavery of the machine, the future of the world depends.[1]

Looking out to midcentury, some experts expect a dramatic existential inflection point in the relationship between humanity and machines that will augur changes, in work and education, of epochal proportions. In that time range (or perhaps somewhat beyond, but certainly within the lifetime of our current students) machine intelligence, they argue, will surpass humans in all or nearly all fields of intellectual production. At that point, there will be very little need for uniquely human input to the workforce. What, then, would provide a sense of purpose to our children in a midcareer world in which they will find themselves, for the first time since *homo sapiens* roamed the African savannah, the second-most capable intellect on the planet?

The utopian promise of this vision—as articulated by futurist Ray Kurzweil, historian Yuval Noah Harari, and others—is that just as automation nips at our heels and threatens to take our jobs, it offers us all the opportunity to live a leisurely life of contemplative and aesthetic engagement. This has, of course, been the dream of visionaries from the Athenian ideal to the Romantic movements of the nineteenth century, and even the counterculture of the 1960s. It is instructive to compare Oscar Wilde's vision cited above with similar pronouncements of the rather less articulate Haight-Ashbury "Diggers" movement of the 1960s, with their assumption that the means of production had reached a stage at which a life of leisure and countercultural indulgence was accessible to all; perhaps the Diggers were merely off in their timing, some decades ahead of actual AI capacities.

In other words, visionaries (quixotic and otherwise) have ever dreamed of a world of abundance in which humans can be freed from drudgery (physical or intellectual) to pursue higher human endeavors, including contemplation of the very cosmos we inhabit. "Scholar," after all, derives from the Greek word for "leisure," and the Greek ideal of a life well lived remains a compelling aspiration.

More recently, a small group of scholars known as "post-workists" has prodded Americans to "welcome, even root for, the end of labor." They cite findings, such as a 2014 Gallup poll, in which as many as 70 percent of Americans said they don't feel engaged by their current job. "Purpose, meaning, identity, fulfillment, creativity, autonomy," University of Iowa historian Benjamin Hunnicutt said, are all "absent in the average job."[2]

Many economists now say that rapidly advancing innovation offers us the chance to experiment with the post-work concept of the guaranteed basic income (GBI), a "citizens' dividend" that we're all entitled to, since our tax dollars make so many innovations possible. "We taxpayers should have a claim on the long tail, in the 'accumulated technological account balance,'" says tech writer Martin Ford.[3]

The idea is actually an old one, proposed as early as 1930 by John Maynard Keynes and championed by both liberals and conservatives—one of its early proponents was Milton Friedman, who proposed a "negative tax" on income; a decade ago, the conservative thinker Charles Murray wrote a book about it.[4] In 1967, the Rev. Martin Luther King Jr. advocated a guaranteed basic income, saying the solution to poverty was to "abolish it directly."

In the late 1960s and early 1970s, President Lyndon Johnson's Office of Economic Opportunity experimented with a negative income tax for 1,300 low-income families in New Jersey and Pennsylvania. An analysis found that it supported them "without deterring them from working." Experiments followed through the 1970s in Seattle, Denver, and Gary, Indiana, but the Seattle and Denver studies found the GBI more of a disincentive for people to work than in the New Jersey study. The findings, a 2016 Mathematica analysis noted, led to the idea's "death knell in the United States."[5]

Fifty years later, a new generation of small GBI experiments command our attention. Facebook cofounder Chris Hughes helped create the Economic Security Project, which states, in straightforward fashion, that cash might be "the most effective and efficient way" to provide people with financial security. "In a time of immense wealth, no one should live in poverty, nor should the middle class be consigned to a future of permanent stagnation or anxiety. Automation, globalization, and financialization are changing the nature of work, and these shifts require us to rethink how to guarantee economic opportunity for all."[6]

In Oakland, California, the Silicon Valley start-up accelerator Y Combinator in 2016 began giving a minimum wage to about one hundred families in a bid to explore "alternatives to the existing social safety net." Elizabeth Rhodes, director of Y Combinator's nonprofit arm, YC Research, noted, "If technology eliminates jobs or jobs continue to become less secure, an increasing number of people will be unable to make ends meet with earnings from employment. Basic income is one way to ensure that people are able to meet their basic needs. We're not sure how it would work or if it's the best solution, which is why we want to conduct this study."[7]

Also in 2016, economists in the Netherlands began a two-year test in which citizens of Utrecht and nearby cities received €960 per month (about $1,100) simply for existing.[8] Results were disappointing. Researchers found the payment actually made poverty worse and had only a small effect on inequality.[9]

In other words, the idea is by no means an easy sell. Voters in Switzerland in 2017 rejected a generous GBI proposal that would have been Europe's first government-backed plan. Fewer than one in four supported it—the proposal would have provided the equivalent of $2,555 to each adult and about $611 to each child.[10]

GBI or no, if humans can somehow fulfill their basic needs, what will they do with their newly acquired leisure? The answer may well determine the future of the species. It is easy to imagine dystopian responses, in which people feel a profound despair at finding themselves redundant to the creative production processes of society and become despondent, nihilistic, angry sybarites.

On the other hand, it is possible to envision a society of poets, mystics, and artists engaged in exploring and expressing the greatest depths of human perceptivity. (This is not even considering what might become possible with human biological enhancement and cyborg-like fusing of human and machine intelligence.)

Could we return to a mid-nineteenth-century conception of employment that includes not just outside work but "home industry" such as sewing, carpentry, and canning? The *Atlantic's* Derek Thompson in 2015 suggested that prior to the twentieth century, even in the worst economic panics, "people typically found productive things to do." He suggested that local governments could create more ambitious community centers, business incubators, and other public spaces "where residents can meet, learn skills, bond around sports or crafts, and socialize," in the process strengthening community pride, entrepreneurship, and small-business formation. Hunnicutt, the University of Iowa historian, has said colleges could reemerge as cultural centers rather than primarily job-prep institutions. "We used to teach people to be free," he said recently. "Now we teach them to work."[11]

How might religious and spiritual cosmologies change? Kurzweil, the futurist, has articulated an interesting new cosmology of human purpose and destiny in which he argues that humans, themselves comprised principally of material forged in stars and released by supernovas that has formed us as sentient beings, are in the process of bringing that very sentience to the entire physical universe. In other words, we are physical matter that has become sentient and are on the cusp of creating physical machines that are similarly sentient; with time, our destiny is to bring this sentience to the entire physical environment. According to Kurzweil, then, humans are the first progenitors in the process of awakening the entire universe to thought and awareness.

One does not have to subscribe to Kurzweil's mystico-scientific vision to recognize in it a breathtakingly sweeping new cosmology that augurs many more such from other visionaries in coming years, with which religious and spiritual thinkers must engage in perhaps unprecedented ways.

What is at stake is nothing short of the self-understanding and sense of destiny humans are to collectively share and realize as we live through the technology revolutions within our lifetime.

To take another recent example, the historian Harari has written that while technology could create a new "unworking class,"[12] further technological tweaks could give the permanently unemployed a new kind of meaning: offer these folks some sort of virtual reality 3-D world in which to play all day. "This, in fact, is a very old solution," he asserts. "For thousands of years, billions of people have found meaning in playing virtual reality games. In the past, we have called these virtual reality games 'religions.'"[13]

What is a religion, he argues, but a "big virtual reality game played by millions of people together?" In a sense, the religious are not just players but "deep players," people who invest so much meaning in a game that it becomes an all-encompassing reality. In Israel, he noted, many ultra-orthodox Jewish men who receive a GBI spend their entire lives studying holy scriptures. "Though they are poor and never work, in survey after survey these ultra-orthodox Jewish men report higher levels of life-satisfaction than any other section of Israeli society," he wrote. In fact, in global surveys of life satisfaction, Israel is almost always among the top, thanks in part to the contribution of these unemployed "deep players."[14]

Could technology give rise to a new spiritual age?

How about a new scientific age, in which connected thinkers, working for free—and for the fun of it—solve tricky problems that bedevil experts? If you don't think people will work for free, consider that unpaid editors around the world tweak Wikipedia's 5.4 million articles more than ten times *per second*, adding about 750 new articles daily. That's just the English-language site.[15]

The crowdsourced online biology game *FoldIt* has shown that people working together from around the world—also for free—can solve complex problems. The game takes advantage of humans' puzzle-solving skills, and harnesses the intrinsic pleasure people take in solving puzzles, to help researchers make advances in treating cancer, AIDS, and Alzheimer's disease, among others, by devising novel ways to fold proteins, a key building block for treating disease. In one of its more well-known challenges, players analyzed a monkey HIV protein whose structure had eluded scientists for fifteen years. A far-flung team of players, working remotely from around the world, figured it out in ten days.[16]

Its successors have equally ambitious goals. The online game *EteRNA* boasts the motto: "Solve Puzzles. Invent Medicine."[17] *Galaxy Zoo*, developed by astronomers to help classify deep sky objects, has enlisted thousands of amateur researchers to classify millions of galaxy images. Its designers initially thought it would take a year to classify the one million images collected by the *Sloan Digital Sky Survey*. But within a day, users were classifying more than 70,000 objects an hour; nearly 150,000 users submitted fifty million classifications in the first year.[18] The project gave rise to *Zooniverse*, a platform supporting citizen research in medicine, climate science, physics, social science, history, languages, and the arts, among others. It calls itself "the world's largest and most popular platform for people-powered research."[19]

To be sure, we consider these GBI scenarios unlikely. Billions of people across the planet, living on guaranteed incomes, compliments of machine-generated surplus, and engaged in crafting, music, and spiritual enlightenment? It seems poetic but a bit far-fetched. One could argue that even today few people need to be employed in providing the necessities of life in advanced societies, yet these societies have created an economic system—and a culture—predicated on most people working in service industry jobs that are largely not, strictly speaking, necessary for material survival.

We also worry that billions of post-work people are more likely to live hedonistic, purposeless lives than flourishing lives of artistic and spiritual endeavor. In other words, for most people, purposeful work is required to live a balanced life. Just so, we believe the current economic, labor, social, and cultural systems are more likely to morph into the *Three Cs economy* mentioned earlier of *creative work*, *cybercurating work*, and, especially, *caring work*.

At any rate, one of the axiomatic goals of our research is to posit an *evolutionized* model for K–12 education that will be germane to *all* of the likely future work scenarios. In this regard, it is worth noting that the educational model described in these pages, particularly a renewed centrality to humanities education within a new context of learning, will prepare students optimally and equally well for the salient features of *either* a post-work world *or* a Three Cs economy—or, indeed, an admixture of both.

Will our education system figure out a way to run with robots or will it stick to the safe, the previously tried (and tired), denying that epochal change is underway? That is perhaps the central question of our day, the answer to which could determine the fate of our democracy and, indeed, civilization itself.

RUMPLE RUMINATES

The car drops Bellamy and Rumple in front of the entrance to a quiet neighborhood restaurant, but, as they emerge, Bellamy says, "First, I want you to peek into this establishment across the street."

She points at what seems to be a performance venue, with blinking lights tracing patterns around a set of large plate glass windows. Above the door hangs a sign that Rumple reads out loud: "'Voluptuous Panic,'" he says. "What the devil?"

"I had to look it up the first time I saw it," says Bellamy. "It's a gaming term, from the mid-twentieth century. It describes the state of mind one experiences while spinning around quickly, a sort of voluntary vertigo. I'm told it also describes what happens to certain endurance athletes, like long-distance runners who tackle treacherous stretches of mountain terrain. Evidently the goal is to lose one's sense of ego and achieve a kind of lucidity that comes from exertion, from the shock and uncertainty of it all. I rather like the sound of it, actually."

"Sounds dreadful," says Rumple.

Bellamy laughs. "Wait 'til you see what's inside."

As they enter, they're met with a blast of sound and light and immediately see that much of the space is taken up with barely separated groups of people wearing jumpsuits and thick pairs of eyeglasses equipped with tiny headsets, taking part in games that only they seem to see or understand.

"I bet you're wondering why the place is packed on a weekday afternoon," Bellamy says.

"Quite right," puzzles Rumple.

"It's interesting. Just as we have developed an elastic sense of being in school, we've developed an elastic sense of work," she says. "Many of these players are between tasks or even between jobs. I dare say, a few are *at* work as we speak."

"At work? How?"

"They're playing games that get work done—problem solving or troubleshooting, all channeled through a virtual world. A few may even be playing on behalf of others who don't have the time or patience to earn in-game rewards and level up—they're proxies who play the dull parts of the game in exchange for cash."

"I've heard of that," Rumple says. "What's it called? Gold farming? I thought it was frowned upon."

"Well, it has taken on a different form in the past few years. The large game studios realized there was money to be made selling convenience, so they developed a kind of secondary auction house system for items of value. In its own way, it's a form of digital craft work, I suppose."

"Fascinating." Rumple looks over at a player who's rather deliberately moving her arms under a neon sign that reads, *Pizza Hero*. He asks, "What's that?"

"Oh," Bellamy says, "*Pizza Hero*. Fascinating story. Several years ago, most restaurants and cafes began replacing their kitchen staff with robots."

"Yes, I remember," says Rumple. "I once got a robot latte in Cambridge."

"Exactly," says Bellamy. "By the way, you'll find that coffee drinks are no longer human-made."

"Really?"

"Quite right. But pizza is another story. Turns out the robots were more efficient at some tasks, but they simply couldn't recreate a real, handmade pizza. That presented a problem. In order to keep costs down, restaurants had to be able to hire remotely. So, some evil genius engineer created a bot that allows a reasonably skilled adult, via a haptic suit, to remotely operate a kind of people-powered pizza bot. That spawned a whole genre of games—they're called Workaways."

Rumple watches as the player massages an imaginary disc of dough, then launches both of her arms in the air and follows the invisible projectile with her eyes, presumably catching it.

"That player is making a pizza for someone, someplace. I have no idea who or where—she probably doesn't either."

"Good heavens," Rumple says.

"For years, one of the most popular Workaways was a sheet-folding game—for all their power and precision, robots for years couldn't figure out how to fold a fitted hotel bedsheet."

"I totally understand why," Rumple says. "It's impossible!" They both laugh.

"Even small children can learn the skill after a few lessons," Bellamy says, "but robots couldn't manage it. Now that type of thing is fast disappearing. Robots have mastered the fitted sheet. Those games are mostly played for nostalgia now, sort of like how my generation once played *Mario Kart*." She looks around the arcade. "Most of these players are here purely for recreation."

"I suppose that's a hopeful development," Rumple says.

"Indeed," says Bellamy. "When you look around the room, it's hard not to notice how far technology has come. It's all quite advanced. The outfits have haptic sensors that simulate all manner of interactions and conditions—hot, cold, wind, rain—even in-game rewards and setbacks." She points to a couple running together on a slick surface that allows them to remain in one place. "I believe that game is *Running with Rhinos*, a popular adventure title that immerses users in an African rainforest from the point of view of its indigenous megafauna. Half the proceeds go to preserving their habitats from deforestation. My students love it."

"And that one, with the players standing perfectly still?"

"I believe that's a guided meditation game. As you can imagine, the past twenty years have seen a big rise in spirituality and enlightenment-seeking. More than ever, people are trying to figure out their place in the universe, their higher purpose."

"What's *that* one?" Rumple asks, pointing to a small group of men wearing ill-fitting suits and the same style of thick black eyeglasses, most with drinks in their hands. They're gathered around a table, though a few stand off to the side. The ones around the table intently talk to one another, as if negotiating. Bellamy and Rumple approach and listen as one of the men says in a strained voice: "Bonasera, we know each other for years, but this is the first time you come to me for help. I don't remember the last time you invited me to your house for coffee . . . even though our wives are friends."

"Oh, that's a *Godfather* simulator," Bellamy says finally.

"A what?"

Bellamy suppresses a laugh. "A few years ago, men of a certain age began endlessly watching and rewatching the *Godfather* movies, learning all the dialogue, acting out the scenes. I don't quite understand it, but a clever game designer came up with a tool that allows players to watch the film in the frame of their eyeglasses, all from the point of view of one of the characters. It digitally inserts them into the film, where they recite the lines on cue—a kind of greenscreen karaoke. The game automatically compares players' performances against the original, then ranks them against one another. There's even an annual award for the best performances."

"Amazing," Rumple says.

"Well, check back in three hours," Bellamy replies. "You can't win the game unless you perform the entire movie."

Now neither can suppress a laugh.

"Come on, let's go someplace a little quieter," Bellamy says.

They duck outside where it takes Rumple a moment to blinkingly adjust again to the late afternoon sunlight. Meanwhile, Bellamy has stepped right out into the street full of traffic, causing Rumple to instinctively reach out to grab her arm and then look up to see if there is a pedestrian crossing signal. Bellamy pats Rumple's arm reassuringly. "Thank you for your concern," she says, "and sorry to forget that you might be anxious about that. There are no streetlights, because the autonomous cars are programmed to stop for pedestrians under all circumstances. Come on. It's perfectly safe."

Bellamy wades confidently out into the traffic, which stops around her as if she were Moses parting the Red Sea. Rumple follows her cautiously.

As they are about to enter the next establishment, a tiny pub filling up with happy hour patrons, Rumple pauses to look up and down the thoroughfare.

"Almost all of the businesses I see are social service organizations," he observes.

"That's right," Bellamy nods. "Very observant. Our own little downtown Winterville is a microcosm of the changes we've been discussing. The caring sector of the Three Cs economy is the largest employer today. But you can see over there," she continues, pointing out a colorfully decorated front to what appears to be an old warehouse building, "a craft- and makerspace business teeming with people who work in the creating sector."

As they enter the pub and approach the bar, Rumple is gratified to see that it's still the old-fashioned kind: mahogany, brass, and high stools, though these are more colorful than the typical barstools, and seem to automatically adjust to the user's height. A young woman approaches, sliding a pair of thick cardboard coasters in front of them.

"A real-live bartender!" Rumple says. The woman gives him a bemused smile.

"Hello, Annabelle," Bellamy says.

"Hello, Ms. B! Who's your friend?"

"A friend from the past," she says. "I'll have a Manhattan, neat. And my friend here . . ."

"Whatever's on tap," he says. "Something local."

Annabelle acknowledges the orders and steps away. Rumple watches as she presses a few buttons on a keypad, then places a dainty cocktail glass and a tall, frosted beer stein beneath a hulking machine that dispenses two simultaneous portions of alcohol. She removes the drinks and slides them into place. His beer is perfectly poured, with a head of foam that just tops the rim of the glass.

"I couldn't find any information on your friend—he really *is* from the past," Annabelle says. "So, I started a tab on your account. That OK?"

"It's fine," Bellamy replies. "We may be here a while. By the way, how's your mother?"

"She's fine, thanks for asking," Annabelle replies. "Those students you sent over—they've been such a comfort. She loves it when they visit."

"The kids are delighted to hear her stories," Bellamy says, then looks to Rumple, lifts her drink and toasts: "To the future."

"May it make better mistakes than the past," he says, lifting his glass.

As they settle in, Rumple notices that Annabelle seems the only actual employee in the place. "Does she handle every-one's orders?"

Bellamy, peering over her glass, says, "Absolutely. The service economy is no longer a major employer. Annabelle is a one-woman show. She owns and runs the place. She even designed the building and had it 3-D printed by a construction bot. Over at the maker space I pointed out, my students actually designed and built the furniture we're sitting on."

"Remarkable."

"In any event," Bellamy says, "the reason I wanted to take you to the place across the street was so you could get a taste of how things have changed in the entertainment world since you fell asleep. You saw just a few examples, of course, but you probably understood what's going on."

"Well," Rumple says, placing his beer on the bar. "The same thing was happening when I began my long nap. Those games certainly leverage our innate desire for challenge, fantasy, and self-improvement—it's all quite aspirational, really. And, if that whimsical *Godfather* game is any indication, quite complex. And cognitively demanding."

"Exactly," Bellamy says. "I've been telling people for years that this is the fate of humans, to forever be seeking bigger, harder, more complex challenges. If the world doesn't bring them to our door, we'll create them ourselves. It makes the teacher's role all the more difficult—and essential."

Rumple thinks about this as he sips his beer. "It strikes me that you're locked into a kind of arms race with places like the arcade. But instead of power, the prize is progress, personal meaning, and self-actualization."

"Yes! It's about who gets to say what learning is. The world is changing so rapidly. If school can't keep up, people will find other ways to learn what they need to learn—what they *want* to learn. Imagine: you and I could be put out of our jobs not by robots, but by a pair of magic glasses and a haptic jumpsuit."

"Well, I for one don't think that would be a great loss," Rumple replies. "The corporations have always been critical of the public schools. If they build a better mousetrap, why not let them sell it to families?"

"Ugh," Bellamy replies, draining her cocktail and signaling to Annabelle for another. "I know you've been asleep for twenty years, but when was the last time you reread Dewey?"

"I'm . . ."

She puts a finger in the air and continues: "'The ultimate aim of education is nothing other than the creation of human beings in the fullness of their capacities.' The aim of businesses is fundamentally different—it's to sell us things." At that moment, her drink arrives, and she thanks Annabelle, then takes a healthy gulp. "Ideally, of course, we're doing both simultaneously: preparing students for capable, responsible citizenship and self-actualization while also giving them the necessary tools to be successful in their careers. If those two somehow intersect, we're in luck. But we shouldn't settle for one without the other," she concludes emphatically.

Rumple, nodding in Annabelle's direction for another beer, considers this. "I see what you mean. And to be honest, I'm a bit disappointed—I thought we'd have solved this problem by now."

"Solved? This is the fundamental dilemma that has always dogged our schools," Bellamy says. "Who are they for, the corporations or the public? Businesses or people? Do they exist for training workers or for training citizens? I don't know that we'll ever resolve that question. Perhaps the best we can do is to keep them in creative tension."

Rumple drains his beer. "You're right that, hopefully, we won't have to choose," he says. "At lunch you said that, after millions of white-collar workers lost their knowledge economy jobs, our schools rescued them. In doing so, I imagine the schools were solving massive social and economic challenges at the same time. Your students are clearly learning to be effective workers while preparing to be good, thoughtful citizens in the process. They're not mutually exclusive. You seem to be doing a good job of having it both ways."

As they reflect on this, Annabelle appears, sliding a second beer in front of Rumple. "You two look like you're solving the world's problems," she says, reaching down and producing three tiny glasses. "This calls for vodka shots—on the house!"

A few more drinks in, Rumple realizes he's audibly yawning—the day has been exhausting, and he tells his companion that he should be heading home, whatever that means. They stand, stretch, and make their way to the curb.

Bellamy says, "I'm going to stay and chat with Annabelle about an upcoming fundraiser. She's also an artist who teaches at our school part-time. Here, I'll call you a car."

She fiddles with her phone, and moments later a tiny vehicle rolls into view and beeps twice. They watch as the door nearest to them pops open. "Come back tomorrow," she says, offering him a bracing hug. "You'll see so much more. I think you'll be pleased."

Rumple returns the hug and says, "I'm so impressed with what you've accomplished. It's not the same old school. It's not perfect, but it is inspiring."

Bellamy helps him into the car and the door closes with a soft click. A panel of lights glows blue and the vehicle speeds off silently. Rumple closes his eyes for the brief trip home. He chuckles to himself thinking about the *Godfather* game. By now, he tells himself, half the players must be dead.

When he opens his eyes, he's somehow back in his bed. The sun is out. He blinks away the light and rises. A tattered paperback book slides off his chest and drops onto the floor. He looks down at the cover: Rousseau's *Emile*.

"Good lord!" he says. "What day is it? What *year* is it?" He checks his watch: 7:30 on a Tuesday morning.

He peers out the window and notices that, instead of the tiny self-driving cars of yesterday, his neighbors' old Fords, Chryslers, and Hondas once again fill their curbsides and driveways. In the spot where that double-wide lounge chair of a car stood the previous night, there is his faded blue Honda Accord—old, faithful, and forever burning oil.

"Was it all just a dream?" he says to himself. "I didn't sleep for twenty years after all. Did I imagine all of it?"

Slightly woozy from the night of drinking—*wait, were there really vodka shots?*—he decides against driving and once again walks the few blocks to school, this time chuckling to himself as he recalls the *Am I drunk?* calculator in that raucous math class. *Was that real? What about those magical creatures in the library? And the Hemingway bot? And Principal Bellamy?*

He arrives, and where yesterday the sign read Winterville THAMES Academy, today it says plain old Winterville High School: his familiar school, a bit careworn and badly in need of a power wash, but still a lovable, solid old three-story brick building.

"There's so much to think about," he says to himself. "So much to consider!"

He climbs the stairs, thinking: *There's a lot of work to be done.*

NOTES

Preface

1. Samuel Pepys' diary, available online at: https://www.pepysdiary.com/diary/

Prologue

1. The concept was most fully explored in *Looking Backward: 2000–1887*, a utopian fantasy novel published in 1888 by the journalist and socialist writer Edward Bellamy.

2. Martin Ford, *Rise of the Robots: Technology and the Threat of a Jobless Future* (New York: Basic Books, 2015), 8. Scott Malone, "Special Report: How Some Textile Mills Sidestepped Armageddon," *Reuters*, June 29, 2010, http://www.reuters.com/article/us-usa-textiles-survival-idUSTRE 65S12220100629.

Chapter 1

1. Sven Birkerts, *The Gutenberg Elegies: The Fate of Reading in an Electronic Age* (London: Faber & Faber, 1994), 31.

2. Birkerts, *The Gutenberg Elegies: The Fate of Reading in an Electronic Age*, xiv–xv.

3. James Bessen, "The Automation Paradox: When Computers Start Doing the Work of People, the Need for People Often Increases," *Atlantic*, January 19, 2016, https://www.theatlantic.com/business/archive/2016/01/automation-paradox/424437/.

4. James Manyika, Michael Chui, Mehdi Miremadi, Jacques Bughin, Katy George, Paul Willmott, and Martin Dewhurst, *Harnessing automation for a future that works*, January 2017, http://www.mckinsey.com/global-themes/digital-disruption/harnessing-automation-for-a-future-that-works.

5. Carl Benedikt Frey and Michael A. Osborne, "The Future of Employment: How Susceptible Are Jobs to Computerisation?" (Machines and Employment Workshop, September 17, 2013), http://www.oxfordmartin.ox.ac.uk/downloads/academic/The_Future_of_Employment.pdf.

6. Landon Thomas Jr., "At BlackRock, Machines Are Rising Over Managers to Pick Stocks," *New York Times*, March 28, 2017, https://www.nytimes.com/2017/03/28/business/dealbook/blackrock-actively-managed-funds-computer-models.html.

7. Martin Ford, *Rise of the Robots: Technology and the Threat of a Jobless Future* (New York: Basic Books, 2015), 115.

8. Richard Susskind and Daniel Susskind, *The Future of the Professions: How Technology Will Transform the Work of Human Experts* (Oxford: Oxford University Press, 2016), 303.

9. Susskind and Susskind, *The Future of the Professions*, 130.

10. Erik Brynjolfsson and Andrew McAfee, *The Second Machine Age: Work, Progress, and Prosperity in a Time of Brilliant Technologies* (New York: W. W. Norton, 2014), 126–127.

11. Andrew Zaleski, "Behind Pharmacy Counter, Pill-Packing Robots Are on the Rise," CNBC, November 15, 2016, https://www.cnbc.com/2016/11/15/duane-reades-need-for-speed-pharmacy-robots-are-on-the-rise.html.

12. Sonali Kohli, Rosanna Xia, and Teresa Watanabe, "Whittier Law School Is Closing, Due in Part to Low Student Achievement," *Los Angeles*

Times, April 20, 2017, http://www.latimes.com/local/education/la
-me-edu-whittier-law-school-closing-20170420-story.html.

13. American Bar Association, *Employment Outcomes as of April 2019
(Class of 2018 Graduates)*, May 6, 2019, https://www.americanbar.org
/content/dam/aba/administrative/legal_education_and_admissions_to
_the_bar/statistics/2018-law-graduate-employment-data.pdf.

14. See Thomas W. Malone, *Superminds: The Surprising Power of People
and Computers Thinking Together* (New York: Little, Brown, 2018).

15. Thanks to mathematician Conrad Wolfram for his explication of
the difference between "the essence of the subject and the mechanics
of the moment." Author interview, September 22, 2018.

16. For more on this, see Code.org founder Hadi Partovi's talk. Hadi
Partovi, "Equipping Students for Success in a Technology-Driven
Economy," EIE17 Keynote, December 1, 2017, https://www.youtube
.com/watch?v=TCTveDTqeWU.

Chapter 2

1. *A Volume of Records Relating to the Early History of Boston, Containing
Boston Town Records, 1814–1822* (Boston: Municipal Printing Office,
1906), 167.

2. *A Volume of Records Relating to the Early History of Boston*, 169.

3. *A Volume of Records Relating to the Early History of Boston*, 172.

4. Emerson would stay just two years, but his successor, Solomon P.
Miles, ran the school for fourteen years. After Miles, Thomas Sherwin
would lead the school for thirty-two years, until his death in 1869.
Emit Duncan Grizzell, *Origin and Development of the High School in New
England Before 1865* (New York: Macmillan, 1923), 43.

5. William J. Reese, *The Origins of the American High School* (New
Haven, CT: Yale University Press: 1999), 36.

6. Theodore H. Sizer, *The New American High School* (Hoboken, NJ:
John Wiley & Sons, 2013), xix.

7. Reese, *The Origins of the American High School*, 248.

8. Grizzell, *Origin and Development of the High School in New England Before 1865*, 5.

9. Stanley K. Schultz, *The Culture Factory: Boston Public Schools, 1789–1860* (Oxford: Oxford University Press, 1973), 19.

10. *A Volume of Records Relating to the Early History of Boston*, 170.

11. Steven Mintz, *Huck's Raft: A History of American Childhood* (Cambridge, MA: Harvard University Press, 2004), 76.

12. Mintz, *Huck's Raft*, 80.

13. William Ellery Channing, quoted in Johann N. Neem, *Democracy's Schools* (Baltimore: Johns Hopkins University Press, 2017), 15.

14. Horace Mann, quoted in Schultz, *The Culture Factory*, 55.

15. Grizzell, *Origin and Development of the High School in New England Before 1865*, 278.

16. Thomas Hine, *The Rise and Fall of the American Teenager* (New York: Harper Collins, 1999), 139.

17. Jurgen Herbst, *The Once and Future School: Three Hundred and Fifty Years of American Secondary Education* (London: Routledge, 1996), 42.

18. Claudia Goldin and Lawrence F. Katz, *The Race between Education and Technology* (Cambridge, MA: Harvard University Press, 2008), 159.

19. Reese, *The Origins of the American High School*, 239.

20. Carl Kaestle, *Pillars of the Republic: Common Schools and American Society, 1780–1860* (New York: Farrar, Straus, and Giroux, 1983), 64.

21. A note of caution is warranted here, as census-takers tended to count entire immigrant (especially Irish) families at this time as "foreign born," even if their children were actually born in the United States. Nonetheless, it is clear that immigrant families, including their native-born children, were constituting more than 50 percent of the urban population in some key American cities on the Eastern Seaboard in the 1850s (including Boston in the Massachusetts 1855 state

census), which fueled strong nativist reaction—notably, the Know-Nothing movement.

22. Kaestle, *Pillars of the Republic*, 163.

23. Calvin Stowe, quoted in Neem, *Democracy's Schools*, 139.

24. Kaestle, *Pillars of the Republic*, 70.

25. Joseph Kett, *Rites of Passage: Adolescence in America, 1790 to the Present* (New York: Basic Books, 1977), 215–216.

26. Sharon Hartman Strom, *Beyond the Typewriter: Gender, Class, and the Origins of Modern American Office Work, 1900–1930* (Champaign: University of Illinois Press, 1992), 2.

27. Strom, *Beyond the Typewriter*, 7.

28. Goldin and Katz, *The Race Between Education and Technology*, 173.

29. Ryan Avent, *The Wealth of Humans* (New York: Penguin, 2016), 54

30. The National Commission on Excellence in Education, *A Nation at Risk: The Imperative for Educational Reform, A Report to the Nation and the Secretary of Education*, United States Department of Education, April 1983, https://www2.ed.gov/pubs/NatAtRisk/index.html.

31. Arthur G. Powell, Eleanor Farrar, and David K. Cohen, *The Shopping Mall High School: Winners and Losers in the Educational Marketplace* (Boston: Houghton Mifflin, 1985), 3.

32. Powell, Farrar, and Cohen, *The Shopping Mall High School*, 4.

33. Powell, Farrar, and Cohen, *The Shopping Mall High School*, 40.

34. Powell, Farrar, and Cohen, *The Shopping Mall High School*, 267.

35. James S. Coleman, "Academic Achievement and the Structure of Competition," *Harvard Education Review* 29, no. 4 (Fall 1959): 337.

36. Philip W. Jackson, *A Life in Classrooms* (New York: Teachers College Press, 1968), 33–34.

37. Jackson, *A Life in Classrooms*, 35.

38. Powell, Farrar, and Cohen, *The Shopping Mall High School*, 306.

39. Powell, Farrar, and Cohen, *The Shopping Mall High School*, 277.

Chapter 3

1. John Markoff, "Computer Wins on *Jeopardy!* Trivial, It's Not," *New York Times*, February 16, 2011, https://www.nytimes.com/2011/02/17 /science/17jeopardy-watson.html.

2. John Searle, "Watson Doesn't Know It Won on *Jeopardy!*" *Wall Street Journal*, February 23, 2011, http://web.nmsu.edu/~jvessel/Watson _Doesn't_Know_It_Won_on_'Jeopardy!'.pdf.

3. Richard Feynman, "The Computing Machines in the Future," chap. 6 in *Nishina Memorial Lectures: Creators of Modern Physics*, ed. Nishina Memorial Foundation, Lecture Notes in Physics series (Tokyo: Springer, 2008), 110.

4. John McCarthy, Marvin Minsky, Nathaniel Rochester, and C. E. Shannon, *A Proposal for the Dartmouth Summer Research Project on Artificial Intelligence*, August 31, 1955, http://www-formal.stanford.edu /jmc/history/dartmouth/dartmouth.html.

5. Luciano Floridi, "A Fallacy That Will Hinder Advances in Artificial Intelligence: Decoupling Problem Solving from Any Need to Be Intelligent Is Key to Breakthroughs," *Financial Times*, June 1, 2017, https:// www.ft.com/content/ee996846-4626-11e7-8d27-59b4dd6296b8.

6. John Markoff and Paul Mozur, "For Sympathetic Ear, More Chinese Turn to Smartphone Program," *New York Times*, July 31, 2015, https:// www.nytimes.com/2015/08/04/science/for-sympathetic-ear-more -chinese-turn-to-smartphone-program.html.

7. Lance Ulanoff, "Microsoft may be running the biggest Turing test in history," *Mashable*, February 5, 2016, http://mashable.com/2016/02 /05/microsoft-xiaoice-turing-test/.

8. The chatbot can be accessed here: https://www.woebot.io/

9. Kathleen Kara Fitzpatrick, Alison Darcy, and Molly Vierhile, "Delivering Cognitive Behavior Therapy to Young Adults With Symptoms of Depression and Anxiety Using a Fully Automated Conversational Agent (Woebot): A Randomized Controlled Trial," *JMIR Mental Health* 4, no. 2 (June 2017): https://mental.jmir.org/2017/2/e19/.

10. Nick Romeo, "The Chatbot Will See You Now," *New Yorker*, December 25, 2016, http://www.newyorker.com/tech/elements/the-chatbot-will-see-you-now.

11. Romeo, "The Chatbot Will See You Now."

12. Romeo, "The Chatbot Will See You Now."

13. James Somers, "How the Artificial-Intelligence Program AlphaZero Mastered Its Games," *New Yorker*, December 28, 2018, https://www.newyorker.com/science/elements/how-the-artificial-intelligence-program-alphazero-mastered-its-games.

14. Somers, "How the Artificial-Intelligence Program AlphaZero Mastered Its Games."

15. Fei-Fei Li, quoted in *AlphaGo*, directed by Greg Kohs (New York: Moxie Pictures and Reel as Dirt, 2017), documentary.

16. IBM and the Institute of Culinary Education, *Cognitive Cooking with Chef Watson: Recipes for Innovation from IBM & the Institute of Culinary Education* (Chicago: Sourcebooks, 2015), 6.

17. Mike Elgan, "The Case against Teaching Kids to Be Polite to Alexa: When Parents Tell Kids to Respect AI Assistants, What Kind Of Future Are We Preparing Them For?" *Fast Company*, June 24, 2018, https://www.fastcompany.com/40588020/the-case-against-teaching-kids-to-be-polite-to-alexa.

Chapter 4

1. Lydia Saad, "Military, Small Business, Police Still Stir Most Confidence," *Gallup*, June 28, 2018, https://news.gallup.com/poll/236243/military-small-business-police-stir-confidence.aspx. (It would be

interesting to see how those results might change were the poll redone at the time of this writing in the summer of 2020.)

2. Claude S. Fischer, *America Calling: A Social History of the Telephone to 1940* (Berkeley, CA: University of California Press, 1992), 22.

3. Fischer, *America Calling*, 157.

4. Fischer, *America Calling*, 164.

5. World Health Organization, *Road Traffic Injuries: Key Facts*, December 7, 2018, https://www.who.int/news-room/fact-sheets/detail/road-traffic-injuries.

6. The Education Trust, *Checking In: Are Math Assignments Measuring Up?* April 4, 2018, https://edtrust.org/resource/checking-in-are-math-assignments-measuring-up/.

7. The New Teacher Project, *The Opportunity Myth: What Students Can Show Us About How School Is Letting Them Down—and How to Fix It*, September 25, 2018, https://tntp.org/publications/view/student-experiences/the-opportunity-myth.

8. Brandon Busteed, "The School Cliff: Student Engagement Drops with Each School Year," *Gallup*, January 7, 2013, https://news.gallup.com/opinion/gallup/170525/school-cliff-student-engagement-drops-school-year.aspx.

9. Indiana University, *Latest HSSSE results show familiar theme: bored, disconnected students want more from schools*, June 1, 2010, http://newsinfo.iu.edu/news-archive/14593.html.

10. The authors are deeply indebted to New America researchers Elena Silva and Taylor White for sharing a draft of their unpublished paper, "What High School Students Need . . . But Aren't Getting," which helped form the basis of much of the thinking in this section.

11. Anthony Bryk and Barbara Schneider, *Social Trust: A Moral Resource for School Improvement* (Chicago: University of Chicago, 1996), 3.

12. Will Richardson, *Why School? How Education Must Change When Learning and Information Are Everywhere*, ebook edition (New York: TED Conferences, 2012).

Why School?

14. Monica R. Martinez and Dennis McGrath, *Deeper Learning: How Eight Innovative Public Schools Are Transforming Education in the Twenty-First Century* (New York: New Press, 2014), 39.

Chapter 5

1. "Cuevas Hits Walk-Off Single in 12th, Hartford Beats Bowie 4–3," *Huron Daily Tribune*, August 16, 2016, https://www.michigansthumb.com/news/article/Cuevas-hits-walk-off-single-in-12th-Hartford-9169177.php.

2. Benjamin Mullin, "The Associated Press Will Use Automated Writing to Cover the Minor Leagues," *Poynter*, June 30, 2016, https://www.poynter.org/2016/the-associated-press-will-use-automated-writing-to-cover-the-minor-leagues/419489/.

3. Paul Colford, "A Leap Forward in Quarterly Earnings Stories," *Associated Press*, June 30, 2014, https://blog.ap.org/announcements/a-leap-forward-in-quarterly-earnings-stories.

4. Joey Marburger, "These Are the Bots Powering Jeff Bezos' *Washington Post* Efforts to Build a Modern Digital Newspaper," *Nieman Lab*, April 26, 2017, http://www.niemanlab.org/2017/04/these-are-the-bots-powering-jeff-bezos-washington-post-efforts-to-build-a-modern-digital-newspaper/.

5. Joe Keohane, "What News-Writing Bots Mean for the Future of Journalism," *Wired*, February 17, 2017, https://www.wired.com/2017/02/robots-wrote-this-story/.

6. Steven Levy, "Can an Algorithm Write a Better News Story Than a Human Reporter?" *Wired*, April 24, 2012, https://www.wired.com/2012/04/can-an-algorithm-write-a-better-news-story-than-a-human-reporter/.

7. Matt Burgess, "How the 11.5 Million Panama Papers Were Analysed," *Wired UK*, April 4, 2016, https://www.wired.co.uk/article/panama-papers-data-leak-how-analysed-amount.

8. Benjamin Mullin, "Bloomberg EIC: Automation Is 'Crucial to the Future of Journalism,'" *Poynter*, April 27, 2016, http://www.poynter .org/2016/bloomberg-eic-automation-is-crucial-to-the-future-of-jour nalism/409080/.

9. Levy, "Can an Algorithm Write a Better News Story Than a Human Reporter?"

10. Will Oremus, "The Prose of the Machines: 'Robots' Are Surprisingly Good at Writing News Stories, but Humans Still Have One Big Edge," *Slate*, July 14, 2014, http://www.slate.com/articles/technology /technology/2014/07/automated_insights_to_write_ap_earnings _reports_why_robots_can_t_take_journalists.html.

11. Author interview, December 21, 2018.

12. Author interview, December 21, 2018.

13. Author interview, January 4, 2019.

14. Author interview, January 4, 2019.

15. Author interview, December 21, 2018.

16. Alex Hern, "New AI Fake Text Generator May Be Too Dangerous to Release, Say Creators," *Guardian*, February 14, 2019, https://www.the guardian.com/technology/2019/feb/14/elon-musk-backed-ai-writes -convincing-news-fiction.

17. Hern, "New AI Fake Text Generator May Be Too Dangerous to Release."

18. Sean Gallagher, "Researchers, Scared by Their Own Work, Hold Back 'Deepfakes for Text' AI," *Ars Technica*, February 15, 2019, https:// arstechnica.com/information-technology/2019/02/researchers-scared -by-their-own-work-hold-back-deepfakes-for-text-ai/.

19. Alec Radford, Jeffrey Wu, Dario Amodei, Daniela Amodei, Jack Clark, Miles Brundage, and Ilya Sutskever, "Better Language Models and Their Implications," *OpenAI*, February 14, 2019, https://openai .com/blog/better-language-models/.

20. Alec Radford, Jeffrey Wu, Dario Amodei, Daniela Amodei, Jack Clark, Miles Brundage, and Ilya Sutskever, "Better Language Models and Their Implications," *OpenAI*, February 14, 2019, https://openai .com/blog/better-language-models/.

21. James Bessen, "The Automation Paradox: When Computers Start Doing the Work of People, the Need for People Often Increases," *Atlantic*, January 19, 2016, https://www.theatlantic.com/business/archive /2016/01/automation-paradox/424437/.

22. Matt Levine, "Fake Accounts Still Haunt Wells Fargo," *Bloomberg Opinion*, October 23, 2018. https://www.bloomberg.com/opinion/arti cles/2018-10-23/fake-accounts-still-haunt-wells-fargo.

23. Johannes Klingebiel, "We All Grow Hooves: 'There's a Lesson to Be Learned Here and It's not about Automation, but Augmentation. Teaming Up with AI, to Become Better, Stronger, Faster. To Become a Centaur,'" *NiemanLab*, January 2, 2019, http://www.niemanlab.org /2018/12/we-all-grow-hooves/.

24. C. Penstein Rosé, R. Martínez-Maldonado, U. Hoppe, R. Luckin, M. Mavrikis, K. Porayska-Pomsta, B. McLaren, and B. du Boulay, eds., *Artificial Intelligence in Education: 19th International Conference, AIED 2018, London, UK, June 27–30, 2018, Proceedings, Part I* (Cham, Switzerland: Springer International Publishing, 2018).

25. See, for instance, presentations at 2018 London AIED conference on "Quantifying Classroom Instructor Dynamics with Computer Vision," "Using Physiological Synchrony as an Indicator of Collaboration Quality, Task Performance, and Learning," and "Student Learning Benefits of a Mixed-Reality Teacher Awareness Tool in AI-Enhanced Classrooms."

26. In the early twentieth century, William Gossett, a mathematician working for Guinness, was asked to improve the brewery's efficiency at ensuring consistently high quality with less sampling from barrels. Gossett devised a statistical method for extrapolating from small sample sets, which was an early and influential contribution to applications as diverse as modern polling methods and cold start algorithms.

27. Kevin Kelly, *The Inevitable* (New York: Viking Press, 2016), 60.

28. See Mitchel Resnick, *Lifelong Kindergarten: Cultivating Creativity through Projects, Passion, Peers, and Play* (Cambridge, MA: MIT Press, 2017).

Chapter 6

1. Author interview, December 13, 2018.

2. Author interview, December 13, 2018.

3. Author interview, December 13, 2018.

4. Monica R. Martinez and Dennis McGrath, *Deeper Learning: How Eight Innovative Public Schools Are Transforming Education in the Twenty-First Century* (New York: New Press, 2014), 3–4.

5. This is a version of Harvard scholar David Perkins' idea that good teachers build curricula in a way that gets students "playing the whole game" of a subject, not just atomized, decontextualized pieces. See David Perkins, *Making Learning Whole* (San Francisco: Jossey-Bass, 2010).

6. Author interview, December 14, 2018.

7. Chris Lehmann and Zac Chase, *Building School 2.0: How to Create the Schools We Need* (Hoboken, NJ: John Wiley & Sons, 2015), xv.

8. Author interview, December 13, 2018.

9. Author interview, December 14, 2018.

10. Author interview, Feb. 28, 2019.

11. Author interview, December 14, 2018.

12. Lehmann and Chase, *Building School 2.0*, 150–151.

13. Author interview, February 28, 2019.

14. Author interview, February 28, 2019.

15. Author interview, February 13, 2019.

16. Author interview, February 14, 2019.

17. Author interview, February 14, 2019.

18. Chris Lehmann, "It's Not Just Kid Behavior," Practical Theory (blog), June 14, 2015, http://practicaltheory.org/blog/2015/06/14/its -not-just-kid-behavior/.

19. Lehmann, "It's Not Just Kid Behavior."

20. Lehmann and Chase, *Building School 2.0*, 72.

21. Lehmann, "It's Not Just Kid Behavior."

22. Author interview, February 13, 2019.

23. Author interview, February 13, 2019.

24. Author interview, August 22, 2019.

25. Nicholas Bostrom, *Superintelligence: Paths, Dangers, Strategies* (Oxford: Oxford University Press, 2014).

Chapter 7

1. Author interview, March 8, 2019.

2. Author interview, March 8, 2019.

3. Author interview, March 14, 2019.

4. Author interview, March 14, 2019.

5. Author interview, March 14, 2019.

6. Author interview, March 7, 2019.

7. Author interview, March 7, 2019.

8. Author interview, March 7, 2019.

9. Author interview, March 7, 2019.

10. Author interview, March 11, 2019.

11. *Somewhere Only We Know*, directed by Kyle Duane Kazimour (Cedar Rapids, IA: Ambivalence Studios, 2018), https://www.imdb.com/title/tt8022802/.

12. Author interview, March 11, 2019.

13. Author interview, March 7, 2019.

14. Author interview, March 8, 2019.

15. See Richard Susskind and Daniel Susskind, *The Future of the Professions: How Technology Will Transform the Work of Human Experts* (Oxford: Oxford University Press, 2017).

16. This model of exceptions managers was inspired in part by Eric Topol, *Deep Medicine: How Artificial Intelligence Can Make Healthcare Human Again* (New York: Basic Books, 2019). The authors borrowed the term "exceptions managers" from a contemporary research hospital using a similar model.

Chapter 8

1. David D. Kirkpatrick, "Army Ousts Egypt's President; Morsi Is Taken into Military Custody," *New York Times*, July 3, 2013, https://www.nytimes.com/2013/07/04/world/middleeast/egypt.html.

2. US Department of State—Bureau of Consular Affairs, "Reports and Statistics," https://travel.state.gov/content/travel/en/passports/after/passport-statistics.html.

3. "Record Number of Americans Hold Passports," VOA News, January 18, 2018, https://blogs.voanews.com/all-about-america/2018/01/18/record-number-of-americans-hold-passports/.

4. Author interview, March 10, 2019.

5. Author interview, March 5, 2019.

6. Author interview, March 5, 2019.

7. Author interview, March 5, 2019.

8. Author interview, February 20, 2019.

9. Author interview, March 5, 2019.

10. Author interview, April 26, 2019.

11. Author interview, March 5, 2019.

12. Author interview, March 10, 2019.

13. Author interview, April 26, 2019.

14. Author interview, April 26, 2019.

15. Author interview, April 26, 2019.

16. You can perform this calculation on your own at: https://www .wolframalpha.com/input/?i=am+i+drunk.

17. David Helfand, quoted in Pippa Biddle, "AI Is Making It Extremely Easy for Students to Cheat," *Wired*, July 5, 2017, https://www.wired .com/story/ai-is-making-it-extremely-easy-for-students-to-cheat/.

Chapter 9

1. Hemingway letter to Arthur Mizener, May 12, 1950.

2. Hemingway letter to Sherwood Anderson, March 9, 1922.

3. Hemingway letter to F. Scott Fitzgerald, May 28, 1934.

4. Hemingway letter to F. Scott Fitzgerald, May 28, 1934.

5. Ernest Hemingway, "Monologue to the Maestro: A High Seas Letter," *Esquire*, October 1935, https://dianedrake.com/wp-content/uploads /2012/06/Hemingway-Monologue-to-the-Maestro1.pdf.

6. Yoshida Kenkō, *Essays in Idleness: The Tsurezuregusa of Kenkō*.

Chapter 10

1. "Max Yasgur Speaks at Woodstock," Political Outsider, video, 2:04, January 10, 2015, https://www.youtube.com/watch?v=8Hfzv04sx4E.

2. Richard Brody, "What Died at Altamont," *New Yorker*, March 11, 2015, https://www.newyorker.com/culture/richard-brody/what-died at-altamont.

3. Alexander Klimburg, *The Darkening Web: The War for Cyberspace* (New York: Penguin, 2017), 26.

4. Klimburg, *The Darkening Web*, 44.

Chapter 11

1. Stanislas Dehaene, *Reading in the Brain: The New Science of How We Read* (New York: Viking, 2009), 302.

2. Plato, *Phaedrus*, 275D–276A, in Edith Hamilton and Huntington Cairns, eds., *Plato, The Collected Dialogues* (Princeton, NJ: Princeton University Press, 1961), 521.

3. Pew Research Center, *Social Media Use in 2018*, March 1, 2018, https://www.pewresearch.org/internet/2018/03/01/social-media-use -in-2018/.

4. Caitlin Dewey, "Who Is PewDiePie, the First Person to Ever Hit 10 Billion YouTube Views?" *Washington Post*, September 9, 2015, https:// www.washingtonpost.com/news/the-intersect/wp/2015/09/09/who -is-pewdiepie-the-first-person-to-ever-hit-10-billion-youtube-views/.

5. Felix Kjellberg, "PewDiePie," YouTube, https://www.youtube.com /user/PewDiePie.

6. "Best-selling book," Guinness Book of World Records, https://www .guinnessworldrecords.com/world-records/best-selling-book-of-non -fiction/.

7. Shelley Fan, "IBM's 'Project Debater' AI Lost to a Human—but Put Up Quite a Fight," *Singularity Hub*, February 25, 2019, https://bit.ly /2XLRbgn.

8. Author interview, April 29, 2019.

9. A video of the debate can be viewed here: https://www.intelligence squaredus.org/debates/ibm-project-debater.

10. Author interview, April 29, 2019.

11. Author interview, March 31, 2019.

12. "*Spore* 35 min Demonstration from the GDCe (2005)," Colin Beirne, video, 35:52, 2003, https://www.youtube.com/watch?v=T8dv MDFOFnA.

13. Author interview, March 31, 2019.

14. Peg Tyre, "The Writing Revolution," *Atlantic*, October 2012, https://www.theatlantic.com/magazine/archive/2012/10/the-writing-revo lution/309090/.

15. Tyre, "The Writing Revolution."

16. Author interview, March 31, 2019.

17. Author interview, March 31, 2019.

18. Author interview, May 19, 2020.

19. Peter Gault, "What Happens When AI Can Write Better Than We Can?" *EdSurge*, April 15, 2016, https://www.edsurge.com/news/2016 -04-15-what-happens-when-ai-can-write-better-than-we-can.

20. Author interview, March 31, 2019.

Chapter 12

1. Oscar Wilde, "The Soul of Man Under Socialism," in *The Complete Works of Oscar Wilde: Historical Criticism, Intentions, The Soul of Man*, vol. 4, ed. Josephine M. Guy (Oxford: Oxford University Press, 2007), 247.

2. Derek Thompson, "A World without Work," *Atlantic*, July/August 2015, http://www.theatlantic.com/magazine/archive/2015/07/world -without-work/395294/.

3. Martin Ford, *Rise of the Robots: Technology and the Threat of a Jobless Future* (New York: Basic Books, 2015), 80.

4. https://www.amazon.com/In-Our-Hands-Replace-Welfare/dp/084 4742236.

5. Paul Decker, "The Idea That Launched a Policy Research Revolution," *Mathematica Center for Improving Research*, June 1, 2016, https://cire.mathematica-mpr.com/commentary/idea-that-launched-a-policy-research-revolution.

6. Economic Security Project website: http://economicsecurityproject.org/.

7. Michael J. Coren, "Y Combinator Is Running a Basic Income Experiment with 100 Oakland Families," *Quartz*, June 1, 2016, https://qz.com/696377/y-combinator-is-running-a-basic-income-experiment-with-100-oakland-families/.

8. Tracy Brown Hamilton, "The Netherlands' Upcoming Money-for-Nothing Experiment," *Atlantic*, June 21, 2016, https://www.theatlantic.com/business/archive/2016/06/netherlands-utrecht-universal-basic-income-experiment/487883/.

9. *Flanders Today* editorial team, "Basic Income Doesn't Work, Antwerp Research Suggests," *Flanders Today*, June 13, 2018, http://www.flanderstoday.eu/basic-income-doesnt-work-antwerp-research-suggests.

10. "Switzerland's Voters Reject Basic Income Plan," *BBC*, June 5, 2016, http://www.bbc.com/news/world-europe-36454060.

11. Thompson, "A World without Work."

12. Yuval Noah Harari, "The Rise of the Useless Class," *Ted.com*, February 24, 2017, http://ideas.ted.com/the-rise-of-the-useless-class/.

13. Yuval Noah Harari, "The Meaning of Life in a World without Work," *Guardian*, May 8, 2017, https://www.theguardian.com/technology/2017/may/08/virtual-reality-religion-robots-sapiens-book.

14. Harari, "The Meaning of Life in a World without Work."

15. Wikipedia: Statistics can be viewed at: https://en.wikipedia.org/wiki/Wikipedia:Statistics#Analysis.

16. Greg Toppo, "White House Office Studies Benefits of Video Games," *USA Today*, February 2, 2012, https://abcnews.go.com/Politics/white-house-office-studies-benefits-video-games/story?id=15485155.

17. EteRNA website: http://ht.ly/dkQDe.

18. John Markoff, "RNA Game Lets Players Help Find a Biological Prize," *New York Times*, January 10, 2011, http://www.nytimes.com /2011/01/11/science/11rna.html.

19. Zooniverse website: https://www.zooniverse.org/.

INDEX

Perkins, David, 246n5
PewDiePie (Felix Kjellberg), 200
Pew Research Center, 200
Pickering, Trace, 125–128
Post-work life of leisure, 5,
    217–224
Poverty, 219–220
Powell, Arthur G., 33–35
Prairie High School (Cedar Rap-
    ids, IA), 121–122
Prakash, Shailesh, 84
Prensky, Marc, 161–162, 166
Professions, traditional, 12
Project-based learning, 103–105,
    108–109, 124–129, 166
Project Debater (computer),
    201–203
Purpose, sense of, 218, 221, 224,
    228

Quantum encryption, 95
Quill, 208–210

Rauws, Michiel, 48
Reading, transformation in, 5–6
Reese, William J., 26, 31
Religion, as a virtual reality
    game, 222
Reynolds, Kimberly, 123, 130
Rhodes, Elizabeth, 220
RHS. See Rocky Hill School
Richardson, Will, 73
Rocky Hill School (RHS; Rhode
    Island), 4–5, 157–175
  admissions at, 163, 169
  collaboration with edtech start-
    ups, 171–174

Hack for Social Good initia-
    tive, 174
innovation at, 159–160, 163–
    166, 169–171
leadership at, 158–159,
    161–162
parents' support for, 162–164,
    173
project-based learning at, 166
reputation of, 162–163, 169
retreats held by, 165–169
soft skills taught at, 166–167
traditional and emerging skills
    taught at, 37
Vision Quest at, 160–162,
    164–165
Rolling Stone magazine, 187
Rolling Stones, 186–187
Roosevelt, Teddy, 2
Russell, Bertrand, 51–52

Scarcity civilization, 1
Schneider, Barbara, 72–73
Science Leadership Acad-
    emy (SLA; Philadelphia), 4,
    103–112
Searle, John, 45
Sedol, Lee, 48
Self-awareness, 51–53
Self-culture, 29
Sentience, 51–53, 221
Shakespeare, William (The Tem-
    pest), 189
Sherwin, Thomas, 237n4
Silicon Valley, 188
Silva, Elena, 72
SimCity, 204–205

World Wide Web. *See* Internet
Wright, Will, 205
Writing/text, 197–200, 203–204,
    206–210

Xiaoice (chatbot), 47
X2AI, 48

Yao Baogang, 47
Yasgur, Max, 185
Y Combinator, 220
YouTube, 200

Zooniverse, 223